085974

W9-DGF-870

A WORLD OF FACES

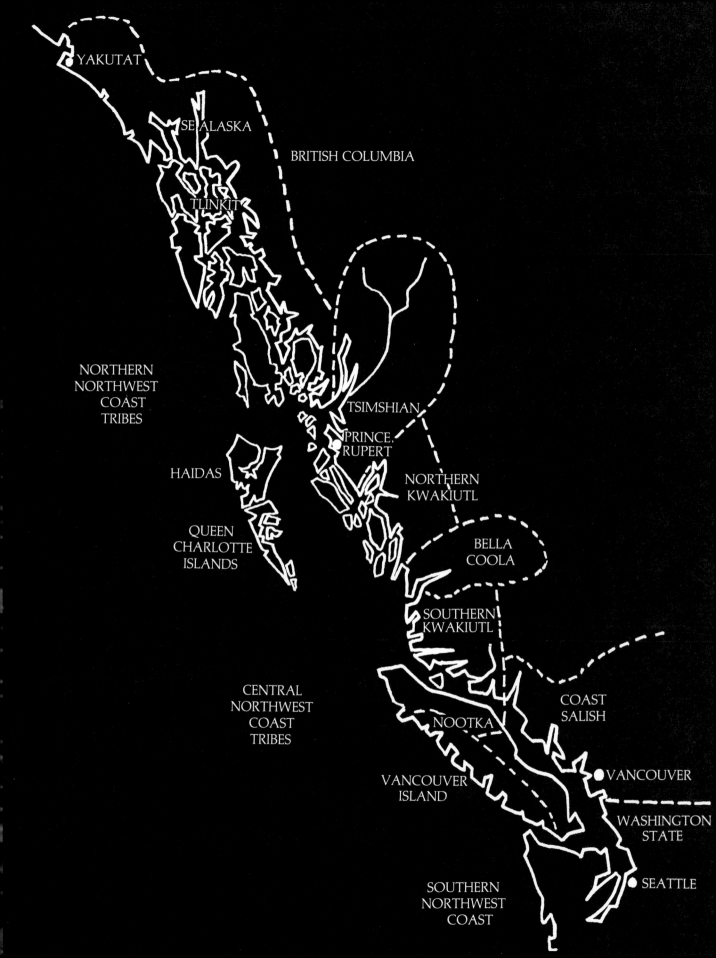

A WORLD OF FACES

Masks of the
Northwest Coast
Indians.

by

Edward Malin
Museum Art School
Portland Art Museum, Oregon

*with line illustrations
in Chapter II and IV
by the writer.*

Timber Press
Portland, Oregon

A WORLD OF FACES

Edward Malin

ISBN 0-917304-03-9

©Copyright 1978 by Timber Press
P.O. Box 10766
Portland, Oregon 97210

LIBRARY OF CONGRESS CATALOGING
IN PUBLICATION DATA

Malin, Edward.
   World of faces.

   1.   Indians of North America—Northwest coast of
North America—Masks.   I.   Title.
E78.N78M34   731'.75   77-26786
ISBN 0-917304-03-9
ISBN 0-917304-05-5 pbk.

PRINTED IN THE UNITED STATES OF AMERICA

This book is dedicated to the late Mungo Martin (Kwagiulth) and to George Nelson (Koskimo), the first carvers to introduce me to the arts of mask making.

TABLE OF CONTENTS

ACKNOWLEDGEMENTS

No one writes a book of this kind by himself. The debt owed to others goes beyond time and space; to informants still living and deceased, to colleagues, scholar-teachers, and friends.

Foremost, I wish to acknowledge my deep and lasting debt to the many Native Americans who shared their knowledge, insights, and points-of-view with me during the seasons I was involved in field research in British Columbia and southeastern Alaska. I would especially like to single out Mungo Martin, Johnnie Hunt, Sam Hunt, and Elizabeth Wilson, all now deceased. In Quatsino Inlet George Nelson, James Walas, Frank Walas, Henry Humchitt, and Charley Clair—each helped me in different ways, but all immeasurably so. To James Sewid of Alert Bay, British Columbia, I wish to express my gratitude for the years of sharing and hospitality. Without all these people's assistance—and many others not mentioned—this book could not have been written.

To two esteemed colleagues, Bill Holm of Seattle and Norman Feder of Sydney, British Columbia, I wish to express appreciation for the years we talked about subjects large and small, expressions of our mutual interest in, and admiration for, Northwest Coast Indian art; to Don Smith of Ariel, Washington, my gratitude for discussions centering around the carver and his problems.

I wish to express my appreciation to The Saturday Review Magazine and Katharine Kuh for permission to quote from her article published in the September 4, 1971 issue.

Last, but by no means least, my deepest expression of thanks to Rachael Griffin, curator emeritus of the Portland Art Museum, who assisted me throughout this venture (and adventure) by acquiring the numerous photographs from the various museums for inclusion in the text; for her encouragement and faith in the ultimate result; and for valuable suggestions concerning the line drawings and text.

With this volume I hope to break new ground in the study of Northwest Coast Indian art. I look forward to new ideas and insights from the generation of students and scholars who follow us.

Edward Malin
Lake Oswego, Oregon
July 18, 1977

CHAPTER I

FACES OF A PEOPLE

The Northwest Coast is that region of North America comprising the southeast coast of Alaska from Yakutat Bay southward, past British Columbia, to the Columbia River country in Washington and Oregon. It is covered from one end to the other with mountains, rugged seascapes, almost uncountable numbers of islands both large and small, rivers and streams, awesome tidal action, and forests seemingly without end. The Indian tribes who inhabited this extensive region for thousands of years developed a way of life based on the seasonal exploitation of the ocean resources which were considerable. These were supplemented by food and raw materials taken directly from the forests.

Until the Russians, following Bering's discovery of Alaska in 1741, began extensive explorations and trading policies with the native peoples, it was a vast unknown to Europe and Colonial America. Contacts between the Indian tribes on the one hand and Europeans and Americans on the other started in earnest in the latter decades of the eighteenth century with explorations by Captain James Cook, followed by numerous others including Captain George Vancouver. Their discoveries brought a host of other explorers flying the flags of many nations, each seeking to extend their country's foothold in the New World or locate the Northwest Passage. The fur trading followed, with increasingly intensive periods of contact culminating in the 1820s and 1830s. Contacts between these distinct cultures were by no means continuously peaceful. They were sometimes amiable, always volatile.

The meeting of these two distinct cultures influenced the Indian tribes on the coast in two momentous ways. First, it stimulated Indian activity and cultural development, causing it to prosper and grow in ways which could not have been foreseen. Each tribe which came into contact with European and American visitors was stimulated by the exchange of trade goods and ideas to the point where the Indians reached new heights in the acquisition of property and wealth—consistent with the ideals of their traditional world.

On the other hand these contacts also laid the groundwork for the disintegration of the Indian way of life, eventually resulting in its utter collapse. We shall focus on this period—a little over one hundred years, brilliant but doomed, a time of both crisis and opportunity, one of the richest, most productive chapters in the world of tribal man in the Western Hemisphere.

Northwest Coast Indian culture, and the sculpture arts which were generated from it, is without parallel or rival in the tribal societies of the world. While parts of West Africa and some regions of the South Seas, particularly that of New Guinea and New Ireland, were potent centers of tribal art, it is the art of the Northwest Coast tribes which rank most effectively with the true masterpieces man has produced, transcending cultural barriers of time, language, and perception.

The roots of this art, deep in the Indian culture of earlier centuries, flowered following the European contacts. Between the first decades of the nineteenth century and those of the twentieth, tribe after tribe experimented, refined, developed and crystallized an art form, a style, and a symbolism which stand as a tribute to man's vision of a sublime communication.

Who were the American Indians living on the Northwest Coast? For the most part their names as we use them now are artificial, phonetic distortions coined for the sake of convenience by European and American travelers and scientists of the nineteenth century. Known collectively today as Tlingit, Haida, Tsimshian, Bella Coola, Kwakiutl, Nootka, and Coast Salish peoples, they probably represent some of the last Asians who made their way across the land bridge to North America. Each group had its own identity and ethos to which was attached a fierce independence and sense of pride.

THE THOUSAND HIDDEN THREADS OF HUMAN CONTROL

Masks have had a prominent place and many roles and functions in the lives of the people of the Northwest Coast. Not to understand them is to limit our understanding of the true nature of their world.

In order to make the masks more comprehensible, and to enable us to appreciate the subtleties of their creation and usage, we must look briefly into the nature of tribal organization of Northwest Coast societies. From the character of the culture we can acquire a glimpse of the life-ways of the various tribes, the shared traits and the distinctive variations.

There are many variables in Northwest Coast Indian life so that it would be a misrepresentation to suggest a general uniformity from one end of the region to the other. But before dwelling on the differences, let us look at the shared qualities.

Rarely in the annals of anthropological literature has there been a culture rooted in a hunting-fishing-gathering subsistence economy which was able to evolve as complex and sophisticated a way of life as that of the Northwest Coast. The entire region depended upon a seasonal inundation of different species of salmon which spawned in the rivers and streams. The salmon seemed without end, coming in relays from February through September, depending on the geography of the coast. Five species followed one another. Salmon was the staff of life, but it was supplemented by other foods in varying amounts. There was halibut, cod, and sea mammals, such as seals, sea lions, and some of the smaller species of whales, all taken with time-proven techniques. There were herring, pilchard, and eulachon. Shellfish were abundant along the many beaches and coves. No one turned up his nose at sea gull eggs, seaweed, sea cucumbers, and the many varieties of waterfowl. And there were deer and mountain goat and other game from the forests. The clement mountains behind their villages provided a wide variety of edible berries, roots, nuts, and fruits. In short there was an abundance of natural and easily collected food not enjoyed by the Indians in the rest of North America.

The forests provided an abundance of easily workable woods as well as fuel for the hearths and for preservation of foods. Techniques were developed for the smoking and drying of various sea foods which preserved their use for months on end. A variety of shells, antler, and stones provided the foundation for a developed technology. Complicated fish weirs, rot-resistant cedar chests, as well as wooden cooking utensils were common examples of their skilled handling of resources. Shells of a multitude of types served a variety of purposes ranging from bartering for goods to use as decorative or functional elements incorporated into their arts. Bone and ivory were skillfully used for utensils. All this and more came out of the abundance of this region.

But man does not live by bread or material goods alone. He is a social creature; he is obsessed with intimations of other and different worlds. These other aspects of human nature lay at the bases of the social structures and institutions, the cultural and religious views and practices—all woven together to order the lives and affairs of the people living within them. They are the threads by which human beings control and shape their social lives.

In few people were these threads so complex and powerful as among the inhabitants of the North Pacific Coast. Few people of a hunting-fishing-gathering society have lived in a social order and religious context as comprehensive and fully defined as the people of this book. An intense and concentrated effort of imagination is required for us—living as we do in an open, pluralistic, pragmatic, scientific society—to comprehend the thousands of intertwined threads of control operating upon the Northwest Coast Indian people.

To present this world in its most marked lineaments I will focus chiefly upon the tribes of the northern and central areas. But the reader must understand an interesting and useful rule when reading the paragraphs which follow—to wit: the northern and central cultural groups had the most elaborate, well defined, and carefully controlled body of institutions, views, and practices in the region. As one moves south these practices become less and less rigid until, in southern British Columbia and Washington State, tribal cultural expressions become pale shadows of their northern neighbors'; we see little evidence of the complex cultural achievements characteristic of the northern areas.

The tribes inhabiting all the coastal areas had little political cohesion. Each went its separate way and viewed itself as elite. The best known groups of the northern coast were the Tlingit, Haida, and Tsimshian (Tsim-shee-an). The Tlingit were comprised of fourteen separate tribes, the best known being the Chilkats, Hoonahs, Hootznuhoo, Stikines, Tongass, Yakutat, to name a few. The Haidas of the Queen Charlotte Islands were grouped into three divisions, the Masset, the Skidegate, and the Kaigani groups. Within each of these divisions were numerous independent tribes which had their own primary villages, Kasaan, Skidegate, Howkan, Skedans, Tanu, Cumshewa, and Ninstints. The Tsimshian of northern British Columbia were divided into three divisions, the coastal Tsimshian, the Niskaes of the Nass River country, and the Gitksan of the Skeena River.

The central divisions consisted of tribes called the Bella Coola, the southern Kwakiutl (Kwa-ki-ootl), and the Nootkans. Like those of the northern groups, these too had numerous tribes. The southern Kwakiutl, for example, were broken down into at least twenty sub-groups which were scattered over a considerable territory. Kwakiutl tribal names such as "people of the eulachon country," "people of the ocean side," or "people of the north country," reflect their aloofness and independence.

The Nootkans occupied all but the northern tip of the west coast of Vancouver Island, with a few tribal offshoots on the western tip of the Olympic Peninsula in Washington State. There were fifteen independent tribes over this dense and trackless territory. Blocked off by the abruptness of the mountain ranges behind them to the east, they were a sea-oriented people whose skills matched those of the Haidas in the North. All these tribes evolved a complex of masked rituals and ceremonies.

Each tribe, regardless of its geographic location, resided in one or more permanent villages. The population of these settlements varied from a few hundred people to a few thousand. The sites of these large villages were usually selected for the protection afforded from the elements, but frequently the location was attributed to the choice of the earliest ancestor who settled there. During the height of fishing and food gathering activities numerous temporary camps were established.

Regardless of the size of the main village the houses were spread out in a single line which paralleled the shoreline close by. The wealthier and more prestigious the dwellers, the larger the house. Some houses were immense, being eighty to one hundred feet in length, forty feet in height, and sixty feet wide. They housed from fifty to as many as one hundred people each.

Inhabitants of each village belonged to a specific lineage house, by which they were identified. Houses were usually named after a traditional symbol, a type of family crest. This crest served as an important rallying point of sentiment and protection.

What were the lineages? They were groups of people who lived together under one household as an extended family. They reckoned themselves as descended from a common ancestor. In the north, house names were taken from the lineage and clan crests. Thus we learn of the whale house, killer whale house, raven house. More colorful names are also found: raven bones house, bear den house, wolf crest house, eagle nest house, or killer whale dorsal fin house.

What did the lineages do? Regardless of what region of the Northwest we are discussing they served very important functions. The people living in them shared food gathering, preparation, and distribution activities. They owned property in common, shared tool and clothing making, and were responsible for each other's conduct. Lineages and clans also had their own religious property of legends, myths, and ceremonial gear.

Among all the northern tribes lineages were part of a larger organizational unit, the clan. Clans were the foundation of every tribe, each being composed of several lineages of varying size. All members of the clan reckoned their descent many generations back to a common ancestor who was not necessarily a human being. The common ancestor might be a culture hero, a deity, a mythical or supernatural being. (This is a significant point to remember.) Clans were unilateral descent groups who practiced strict exogamy, marriage between members of the same group being strictly forbidden.

Beyond the clans were larger organizations—combinations of clans, moieties (halves of tribes), phratries (groupings of clans into units), and on and on—all complicated and of little concern to us at this time, except to indicate the complexity of the society. Suffice it to say that all these organizations also had crests and crest names; frog-raven, killer whale, eagle, wolf, etc., and these were viewed with respect and awe as sacred entities.

The clan organization among these tribes had a powerful grip on its membership. Birth into one or another of the clans determined one's role irrevocably throughout life to the grave. It dictated how one behaved towards others, the kinds of language used to address others, whom to refrain from speaking to (out of respect), whom to avoid, whom to support, and whom to defend in times of crisis. It regulated whom you lived with, where your children lived, and who educated them. It even determined where and with whom you were buried. A husband and wife, for example, who had shared a long marital life together were not buried together. They came from different clans and in death were buried with their respective kin groups. Kinship ties remained in force regardless of what else a person did.

In the central region lineages were more characteristic of tribal organization than clanship but, like the clans, lineages had their requirements of members, i.e. loyalties, obligations, commitments. A lineage controlled the relationships between tribal members and owned considerable property, including the rights to streams and rivers, salmon spawning grounds, and food gathering areas. As with the northern groups, there was considerable jockeying among the lineages for leadership, particularly with regard to the acquisition of positions and privileges which brought it high status and honor. Unlike the tribes of the north which practiced a unilateral matrilineal descent system, the tribes in the central region preferred the more flexible bilateral reckoning of descent.

This brief outline of social structure only suggests one facet of the close relation between human organization and the Indian world view. To understand fully not only the rituals but also the place of masks in this society, it is necessary to limn out the religious world and trace the other invisible threads which controlled the life of these people.

No thing or creature in the physical world was without animus or spirit. Every act, however seemingly commonplace, had to be done with proper care and respect and within the rules of a received tradition designed to cope with all aspects of an uncertain world.

A rock could only be picked up in a defined way, lest the life-force in it, offended by improper handling, bring some evil on the offender.

The Salmon Bringer would not lead the salmon to run if not properly propitiated and persuaded.

Disease was the action of some evil influence which the shaman had to identify in trance and draw out of the victim with healing rattles and masks.

Spirits must be mollified.

The dead must be placated.

Careful ritual must be used to prevent destructive storms, placate the spirits of the forest, and prevent the demons in and out of the sea from thwarting the plans of men.

Accustomed as we are to much freedom of choice and a largely benign natural environment, this world seems alien. We must place it all in proper perspective. The old adage holds: he who has more hair to comb has less face to wash. There were many compensations for these people despite the seemingly stifling character of this psychological environment. None ever had the experience of feeling alone, isolated, or destitute in the world. Membership in a clan or lineage gave each person a sense of security little known in our society. A person had allies he could turn to for help throughout his life. In times of stress, kinsmen stood ready, whether the need was financial, moral, protective, or otherwise. A total commitment was expected.

THE DAILY LIFE OF THE NORTHWEST INDIANS

Northwest Coast Indian life, with its base of abundant foods and material resources, was unlike that in any other region in America. It was also a geographically isolated region. The immensity of the mountains and the denseness of the forest cover discouraged continental communication to the east, while it was easy to move northward and southward along the coastal routes. A maritime way of life evolved that had its own distinctive stamp.

Other peoples of the world have lived in isolation; others have had abundant food resources, particularly those living by the sea. Why did these tribes evolve differently? No one can say for certain. No one has been able to explain satisfactorily the underlying urge of a people to follow one particular course rather than another.

A striking characteristic of the Northwest Coast Indians is their pre-occupation with *doing*. They seem to have been by nature an industrious people. With food available in profusion, leisure became common-place and they filled it; they chose the course of "doing things."

They made things and accumulated possessions. Women worked at weaving garments and basketry-making, gathering barks, searching out roots, drying beach grasses, stockpiling mosses to be used as dyes. The men had a predilection for tools. Tools were created out of the widest variety of materials: ivory, stone, antler, bone, wood, hides, shells, even teeth from animals. They invented varying forms and hand holds and developed motor skills. With these efforts came a wide range of experimental perceptions, a curiosity about technical proficiency, and adaptation of form to function. Every man was a craftsman; a much smaller number aspired to be artists, and their greater gifts were recognized.

The men had a preoccupation with mechanical contrivances. They made fish weirs, leisters, and fish hooks of different patterns and from woods with different strengths and durabilities, enabling them to snare a variety of fish and molluscs with differing undersea habits. Tools were models of efficiency.

Canoes, whether ten or forty feet in length, were made with the patience and craftsmanship of naval designers. Tools were fashioned to measure, scoop out, probe, or test. Western red cedar beams, tons in weight, were raised. Houses which have withstood the ravages of rain, wind, dampness, and rot for one hundred years, and more, were built. Marvelous bent wood containers in a variety of sizes were built for the storage of food and ever-increasing amounts of property. No one in a hurry, but every one doing something.

While the Coast Indians looked at a natural world with its infinitely changing patterns and colors, a world well worth looking at, if they wondered about and speculated on its significance in their lives, that did not stop the work. Restless hands and probing minds. Each tribe competing, each tribe trying to broadcast its character and its net worth.

The second distinctive pattern was a pronounced acquisitive bent. They stockpiled possessions of all kinds. This wealth consisted of two distinct kinds, the material wealth that was expendable and the incorporeal wealth that lasted forever. The latter was comprised of songs, myths, dances, crests, names, and positions of honor within the tribe. Gradually this incorporeal wealth assumed paramount importance. A tribe's goal was to climb the ladder of success, to acquire more rights and privileges through inheritance or marriage, preferably both. With the Northwest Coast Indians the higher the position, the greater the hunger for more rights and more honors. All enhanced the group's name.

As the flood of trade goods and coveted new items were introduced by outsiders—goods with a novelty and in a quantity the Indians had never dreamed of before—this passion for acquisition was stimulated, escalating to a near frenzy.

THE POTLATCH CEREMONY

A person accumulated wealth and then acquired honor and prestige by being magnanimous, giving lavishly to those outside his own tribe. One gave wealth away publicly. The tradition of giving wealth to others not of one's own tribe or clan must surely be very old among the Northwest Indians. It is a widely shared characteristic of all North American Indians. Giving and acquiring vast fortunes of goods became the *raison d'etre* for both individuals and villagers. No one, after all, wanted to be known as being stingy.

Giving wealth stimulated rivalry between clans, groups, and tribes as each tried to outdo the other. Some tribes like the Tsimshian and southern Kwakiutl eventually went to extremes in property giveaways. These formalized occasions are called potlatches.

There are no two authorities, it seems, who agree on the evolution and exact function of potlatches. But all agree it was at the root, the heartbeat as it were, of Northwest Coast Indian life. One thing is certain. The institution had a long and complicated history reflecting many changes over long periods of time, with each tribe's practices evolving in a slightly different way. Tlingit and Haida Indians potlatched more to honor deceased leaders and to institutionalize a successor or heir. Tsimshian and Kwakiutl potlatched to settle competing claims for coveted positions, or to confer prerogatives that went with them. In extreme forms, potlatches were vehicles to settle grudges or to best rival groups, in an effort to make one's group pre-eminent. Among the Salish and Nootkans these extreme activities did not become entrenched.

All leaders aspired to potlatch. One group led by its leader, who was the host, invited several outside groups as guests. Guests frequently numbered in the hundreds. The host displayed his hereditary possessions, privileges, songs, dances, and masked performances—in other words the possessions attached to his position. A new name and rank might be claimed if it was vacant in the tribal structure. The potlatch ended with a vast distribution of gifts and the feeding of all the guests present. The aspect of payment and distribution of wealth to guests who were formal witnesses to the proceedings helped validate it for the host. Some experts write that it served to raise the prestige of a group; others say it didn't raise anything. It merely confirmed what one already had claim to.

Potlatches took many forms, proliferating in some areas and being less frequent and more modest in others. There were potlatches to validate claims to positions as chieftains and to elevate men into secret ceremonial societies. There were mortuary potlatches commonly found in the northern area but also in the central region. Other potlatches redeemed brides, a woman's bride price being returned to her husband many years after the marriage. It was a very honorable thing to do and even today remains the goal of many illustrious elder women. There were face-saving potlatches to eradicate the stigma of an embarrassing incident which had, unfortunately, been witnessed by others. On rare occasions there were potlatches to control malcontents.

Conspicuous consumption of goods was common at potlatches which sometimes lasted weeks on end. Gift distribution was extravagant and each gift was given according to the recipients position and rank. Wealth was on occasion wantonly destroyed "as a show" among some tribes. Hosts hired special speakers to recite family histories and events. Potlatches were hosted by chiefs or high ranking members of a tribe as well as those who aspired to that position through potential hereditary rights. One never invited one's kinsmen as guests. They worked on behalf of their leader in the potlatch.

Potlatches were dramatic affairs, conducted with many surprises and with great intensity. Occasionally potlatches erupted in quarrels over protocol or assumed insult or slander, some of which may have contributed to the entertainment value. The dramatic aspects brought to the fore numerous characters in costume and masks who enacted incidents from the past which the rich folklore and mythologies of each tribe provided. Thus emerged in visual form a complex series of ceremonial events which revealed the host's supernatural forebears. The artists made all of it impressively visible.

A WORLD OF FACES

The art most popularly associated with the Northwest Coast Indians is the carved wood column of cedar called the totem pole: poles covered with carved faces from top to bottom, faces representing all kinds of creatures derived from their worlds as they conceived them.

But it is the faces that were carved into the masks that command our greatest attention. The masks collected in the latter half of the nineteenth century and now residing for the most part in museum collections provide us with valuable keys which can unlock secrets, enabling us to understand the culture of the Northwest Coast tribes. Masks were the real treasures, the most valued and prized of all possessions of these people.

The viewer of Northwest Indian carving must have many questions: why all the faces in such limitless variety? What do all of them mean? What do they tell us, a people from a vastly different culture?

All of us find human faces fascinating to watch. They reflect the full range of life's experiences. Travel anywhere, within one's own city or to other lands, the first impact we feel is that of the faces, and the mannerisms, of the inhabitants. They express the full gamut of human emotions, experiences, and needs. Tribal man was keenly aware of the power inherent in the human face. Artists worked to capture the nuances of life reflected in the faces of their kinsmen or their enemies, catching both the visible and inner qualities, to reveal a singular truth. But different cultures think of faces in different ways. On the Northwest Coast, Indians developed a tradition of providing a face for every object in their material world, be it inanimate or animate. Boulders or islands off the vast coastline had faces, as did seawater, kelp, and seaweed. And of course ghosts, spirits, and demons had faces. The Indian material culture, the accoutrements necessary for daily living, was filled with depictions of faces. Whether objects were of a mundane nature or of a lofty spirituality, the artist gave them faces. Faces were everywhere.

The variety is endless. There were faces that served no functional purpose other than decoration, as space fillers in a design. There were faces with deeply etched spiritual content. There were faces on the smallest functional object: fish hooks, net sinkers, fish clubs, even the handles of tools. There were faces carved on weapons and on household objects, like bowls to eat from and spoons to eat with. There were faces on boxes large and small used for the storage of food or to house valued ritual paraphernalia. There were faces on drums which had ceremonial use, faces on baskets and mountain goat wool blankets, faces on canoe prows and paddles, water bailers, or boxes containing magical charms. There were faces on staffs and rattles used for dances, faces on cedar wall paintings, faces on totem poles. And there were masks.

The masks are the objects which have the greatest power, the greatest impact on the viewer. How fertile the imagination of a people who could create such an endless variety of images! Never two masks alike, yet they number in the thousands. There were masks for religious uses and masks for profane uses, those worn for secret ritual experiences and those for social purposes, those denoting great solemnity and others for just plain fun. There were masks worn to heal the sick or provide security in times of uncertainty, to drive away forces threatening the health of man, and those which helped enact stories of his origins. Masks revealed the evidence of man's journeys to strange unearthly places; others evoked mirth and enjoyment. In their wide variety they served almost every human need. The Indians of the Northwest Coast lived a wide ranging emotional life from deepest religious communion to explosive joy, times when spiritual forces come close to man, and also the moments when man reached for union with his fellow man. In this world of faces there are small masks and large ones, masks in profile and masks in full view, masks with hands and feet attached and others with smaller faces surrounding a large one. There are single-faced masks and double-faced masks; janus-type masks, masks within masks, and masks with three, four, or even five faces. Masks had happy countenances or fierce, terrifying ones; faces expressive of fear or anguish, or images of a trancelike state. The masks enabled the impersonator to transform himself as if by magic; indeed, it was all magic!

Transformation was a magical process that was possible for all living creatures of the world, a kind of metamorphosis as from cocoon to moth, from flesh to spirit, from animal to human being or from the human to the god-like. Fortunate indeed are those few who have been allowed to see these masks in action, as they were intended to be seen, in deeply moving dance-dramas performed by the leading members of the clan in an atmosphere of high emotional tension created by the audience of the clan members anxious for success and critical rivals hoping for failure, all enacted before monumental house posts and house screens, in the flickering ambiance of glowing coals left from lively cedar fires.

When we look at the masks in the museum collections, we have to imagine this vital world which once existed. Masks were never intended by their creators to be seen behind the glass protection of galleries and exhibition halls. We must use our imaginations to place the masks in the dark and dripping rain forests of the coast, tuning our hearing to the pitch of wind, cascading streams, and pounding surf, smelling the pungent smoke of the longhouse hearths. Then we can move a little closer to the world of the masks.

THE FLOWERING OF MASKS

The flood of trade items which reached the coast in the late eighteenth and early nineteenth centuries gave the Indians easy access to knives, nails, chisels, and axes made of iron. Other materials such as canvas, cloth, buttons, and paints also became available. Traditional, laboriously-made tools for carving were gradually discarded in favor of superior implements or novel materials. The men were quick to grasp the uses to which metal tools could be put, and they acquired them in profusion. Blades were reshaped, axes were redesigned to fit traditional patterns of carving. Metal tools facilitated carving to the point where demands on the artists' productivity increased, given the competitive nature of the societies. Artists were spurred to innovate, to astonish and awe the viewers of a patron's history at an important potlatch. Each effort pushed back horizons of the artist's perception, and they revealed with increasing clarity and skill the nuances in their assignment. Metal tools unleashed the artist's capacity to produce more easily, to express bold new ideas, and contrive experiments, which fueled the fires of competition between rival tribes.

More and more apprentices flocked to established carvers to take up the challenge of mask making. A veritable explosion of masks followed. Northwest Coast society crystallized into a culture of specialists: those who carved dugout canoes, others who carved totem poles, those who specialized in box making, household items, ceremonial paraphernalia, and masks and costumes.

But behind all this activity were forces inimical to the mask-making arts and to the institutions closely associated with their use—particularly potlatching and secret society ceremonies. The values, perceptions and practices of the Indians came into direct conflict with those that represented Western Civilization. The well-being of the Indians was the rationale for their conversion and control by western forms of government. Whites, some of whom were well-intentioned enough, were guided by the view that Indians should be rescued from heathenism and "civilized."

The flowering of the arts on the Northwest Coast occurred as the seeds of their cultural destruction were being sown. Governmental policies and missionary zeal sought to undermine and eradicate tribal culture, replacing it with Western political, religious, and social institutions.

Despite the missionary efforts and governmental pressures to stamp out traditional arts and institutions, the policy was only partly successful. Tribes responded to these pressures in different ways; some capitulated *en masse*, others changed their outer trappings while practicing some of their customs *sub rosa*. A few resisted conversion and change with desperation by retreating to isolated locations.

But there were other enemies to face, and these weakened the resistance of the Indians. The population declined drastically as diseases were introduced for which the Indians had developed no immunity. The economic subsistence base became undermined. Mask making, dances, and potlatching were forbidden. Gradually in the extreme northern and southern sections of the coast these practices collapsed and disappeared. In the central region isolated pockets continued to practice traditional rituals, masks continued to be carved, and their ownership and pride in them continued to be passed from generation to generation. The momentum created by the demand for masks in the nineteenth century flowering, and the concomitant prestige and influence associated with their ownership, had developed a thrust of such magnitude as to resist the total obliteration of this traditional craft. This is testimony of the masks' spiritual hold on the people of the region. There is every reason to believe that the practice is not only not moribund, having refused to die out, but that it may be destined to be revived with greater vitality and creativity than has previously been thought possible either by experts or by the Indian people themselves.

CHAPTER II

HOW THE MASKS WERE MADE
AND USED

Northwest Coast Indian carvers made masks relating to every aspect of the physical and spiritual fabric of their societies. There was apparently a need which could not be denied for portraying their lives in faces of every imaginable shape and form. These masks may appear foreign to us, but they have an undeniable power to communicate to us whose beliefs and perceptions are so far removed from theirs. Who were the carvers who created such powerful forms and what were the sources of their inspiration?

Carvers had to orchestrate and then translate in tangible form the hereditary symbols, beliefs, and social institutions provided by leading members of the lineages and clans. The products the carvers created were then given life in the tribal extravaganzas called potlatches, or in religious rituals. Chieftains and other leaders provided the stimuli and directions through the tales they told, the visions they inspired, and the rewards they distributed.

Until relatively recently mask carvers were anonymous individuals both by intention and behavior. Therefore, information about them is extremely scanty. Carvers were little known outside their own tribe. Save for a very few notable craftsmen, they commanded little attention or interest elsewhere. Of the thousands of masks in museums there is only a handful which can be identified with a particular carver. Only a few masks contained in this volume can be attributed to a specific carver with any degree of certainty.

Therefore, the names of only a handful of master carvers have been handed down and surprisingly little is known even of these few. When museum curators and art connoisseurs began collecting examples in the early nineteenth century, their attention was focussed on the objects themselves rather than on the men who made them. Little information was collected on mask makers at work or their tools, techniques, and skills. My approach is based on numerous field trips and interpretive studies of the masks. It does not follow that the techniques and skills described below were necessarily those used by the early masters or by all the carvers within the Northwest Coast culture. We can, however, make reasonable inferences from studying the techniques that are still being used.

APPRENTICESHIP AND TRAINING OF A CARVER

With rare exceptions mask carvers were grouped into a profession that was restricted to high-status males who held leading positions of rank within the tribe, though few were chieftains. Commoners were barred from mask making because their low status precluded entry into the secret societies whose members employed masks. Only persons possessed of a lineage enabling them to rise to positions of prominence within the tribe were accepted as apprentices. Only by way of their ascribed status could they be exposed to the secrets of the masked rituals and thus be allowed to carve them.

The Northwest Coast tribes were organized along lines of hereditary rights which included the rights to do carving. If either parent was related to an established carver, the child could claim the right to learn to carve. In this way two famed Kwakiutl carvers to whom I shall refer frequently, Charlie James and Mungo Martin, both claimed rights to learn carving through descent on their mothers' side.

A carver of masks was a product of his tribe and culture. He was indoctrinated into its values and standards and became one of the principle guardians of its traditions. But the people of the tribe set the standards for the acceptance or rejection of the artist's work, and the final judgment of its worth rested in their hands. The good carver understood the power of tradition; he recognized the boundaries between freedom and restraint, conformity and nonconformity, and he trod the thin line between those extremes, searching for his own creative style, drawing upon an imagination steeped within his heritage. He rejected aberrations of form because the unusual could not communicate in the traditional context. If his work failed to communicate, tribal censure and the end of his career as a carver were sure consequences.

On the other hand, the carver was no mere automaton, a copier of the past, imitating the forms of his teacher. Examination of masks made over a long period of time discloses continuing change both in style and substance. But there is always continuity, a thread tying one mask with another, and all have a distinctive Northwest Coast stamp. There were innovators within this carving framework; men such as Mungo Martin and Charlie James were powerful trend setters, generating new ideas and expressing themselves both in the sculptured forms and the painted surfaces of the masks. Willie Sewid, the Kwakiutl, created new forms in ritual masks such as the crooked beaks, deviating from established practices, but never so markedly as to invite condemnation from the elders.

Families watched a son or nephew who revealed a talent for carving. He was encouraged to pursue such interests. Eventually arrangements would be made to place the young man in an established carver's household as an apprentice. Payment for such services were agreed upon and the relationship, once established, often lasted for many years. When the apprentice had acquired sufficient skill he was free to leave his teacher and work independently.

Instruction consisted of familiarizing the apprentice with the tools of the trade, the variety and character of the woods available, the techniques and mechanics of carving. He had the opportunity to examine and become familiar with design symbolism, color preferences, and aesthetically pleasing surface textures. But most of all, the apprentice was encouraged to watch carefully, listen, and follow his teacher's instructions. Blocks of wood were given to him to experiment with. He was encouraged to make his own tools so that they fit his hands comfortably. As he made progress he might be given a part of a secular mask to complete for the teacher's patron. Repetition, observation, experimentation, and controlled participation were integral parts of a training period.

An indispensable element in the training of every successful apprentice was instruction in a complex and detailed code of behavior, rituals to follow, special songs to sing when using particular tools or carving in specific ways. He was given magical potions to help him deal with malignant forces. Certain behavior was proscribed because of inherent dangers, to him and others. Continuing and close attention to the regulation of his daily life was required to protect himself, to assure success, and to increase his power to carve well.

In addition it was necessary for the young apprentice to build the strength of his hands, wrists, and arms. Without such strength one could not be a carver. Carving a mask required tremendous control of both wood and tools. It is far easier to carve a large heraldic pole than a mask because of the skill and attention needed to execute the subtlety and detail in the latter.

ARTISTS AND PATRONS

After years involved in acquiring the secrets of his craft, an apprentice might strike out on his own. Each tribe had but a few practicing mask carvers of merit at any one time due to the strict entry requirements, the long apprenticeship, and the skills and aesthetic sensibilities required. Even so, carvers did not make a living from their professional skills alone. Carving was not a full-time, year-round occupation. A carver was not a person set apart from others of his tribe either by dress, language, possessions, or mien. A man was recognized for his special abilities, but he lived much as others lived, following traditional subsistence activities such as hunting and fishing, and meeting normal obligations to the group. But a gifted carver was respected for the power he acquired, power to see what others could not see, and power to transform what they were unable to transform.

When a patron, a chief of means or a high ranking member of the tribe, required new masks in order to undertake a potlatch or to participate in a masked ritual, a search for the proper carver was begun. Negotiations were generally held in secret as part of an overall strategy of surprise. The order for masks might precede the actual performance by several years. The chosen carver was invited to come to the home of his patron, the finest of hospitality being extended to him for the necessary period. The patron and carver spent much time consulting, as the patron narrated and personally dramatized the extraordinary events of his family's history or the meaning of a religious activity. Family crests were explained, sequences of acquisition of crest properties given in detail, allowing the artist to visualize the episodes required for masked portrayals. Since the patron was a person of immense prestige and stature, often occupying the highest rungs of his tribe's social ladder, it was a momentous time.

Patrons were remarkable people under any circumstances. By tradition they embodied the noblest attributes of their ancestors. They were men of substance and wealth. . .and custom required them to share such wealth with others in an open-handed, completely unselfish way. They held the highest of tribal honors, positions, privileges, and rank. Not only did a patron tell the carver of his great ancestors but he acted out the narrations, singing the treasured songs in their proper contexts, describing the characters involved, the action, and the miraculous conclusions. There was little self-consciousness—this was communication in its most intense, dramatic form. A carver came to understand his patron's most cherished traditions with a special intimacy.

These experiences were locked within a carver's memory. Long intensive exposure has a cumulative effect. Little wonder the established carvers of the Northwest Coast tribes had reputations for their animated story-telling skills and were frequently superb composers of songs, also remarkable singers, dramatic actors, dancers, poets.

A patron cared little for the expense involved in acquiring masks. He was concerned only with the honor and prestige that would accompany the presentation of such properties within their proper contexts. To create impact and surprise were the goals. The patron required of the carver masks providing startling effects which would elicit strong responses, mesmerizing viewers and sending quivers of envy into rivals. The carver was paid according to his patron's position; there was never a fixed price for anything. The higher the patron's status, the more he was expected to pay. By the same reasoning, the patron found it to his interest to pay exorbitantly for an outstanding mask—it would make his prestige soar.

On the other hand, while the carver of the masks for a successful performance was paid handsomely, the more important considerations for him were that he was privy to extensive esoteric knowledge; that he had the challenge of a new and complex problem; and that he acquired prestige for its successful resolution, thus meeting the patron's expectations. The carver never used the masks he created; that honor was reserved for kinsmen of the patron. Rewards were in watching the audience as well as the patron's response to the impact of the masks. Not infrequently the carver sat inconspicuously in the audience watching the performers manipulate the masks. A successful carver had much to be proud of, and he could expect visits from other patrons who had commissions in mind.

Certain tribes distinguished between carvers of secular objects and carvers of sacred or ritual materials. The Tsimshian, for example, assigned lesser status to the totem or heraldic pole carvers than to the makers of masks for secret rituals and potlatches.

THE MECHANICS OF CARVING

Tools: Carvers employed distinctive tools which, in terms of design and function, have roots deep in antiquity, hundreds, even thousands of years ago. Iron-bladed counterparts were introduced in the late eighteenth century by European explorers and traders. A direct tie can be discerned between the older tool-forms and the more recent adaptations.

Traditional tools were adzes made with serpentine or jadeite stones, one end of which was ground down to an edge; stone mallets or hammers, animal tooth knives (particularly beaver teeth); and antler chisels. Iron tools used by the Northwest Indians have changed little over the last 200 years, revealing a basic conservatism with regard to tool types. But carvers were quick to adopt other tools like iron groovers, chisels, saws and fros which provided new effects or facilitated their efforts.

Adzes of various kinds were the principle tools of the carver. The carver could hardly have done without them for they were used to rough the work out of a piece of log. Knives were reserved for the final carving, trimming, and finishing of a mask.

Among the most important tools were the traditional D-shaped (Figure 1) and elbow adzes (Figure 2). Chisels of antler of iron in their traditional form were used but straight bladed knives were adapted to carving needs when metal knives were introduced by Europeans. The metal blades were heated, then bent into various curves to produce an elemental carving tool called the crooked knife. Carvers employed both left and right-handed knives as well as blades sharpened on both edges so they could be used ambidextrously. Some blades had extremely abrupt curves while others had slightly modified curves.

Carvers used straight-bladed pocket knives (Figure 3) when working straight, shallow surface cuts. The crooked knives (Figures 4, 5 and 6) provided easy access to the surface curves so characteristic of face masks. Every carver had a tool box in which he stored a variety of carving materials. Mungo Martin, the Fort Rupert carver, for example, had as least half a dozen large and small elbow adzes, several D-shaped adzes with different blade widths, and dozens of crooked knives, each having distinct functions and uses.

The more subtle characteristics of tool design are not always apparent. The elbow adzes, for example, have different striking blade surfaces,

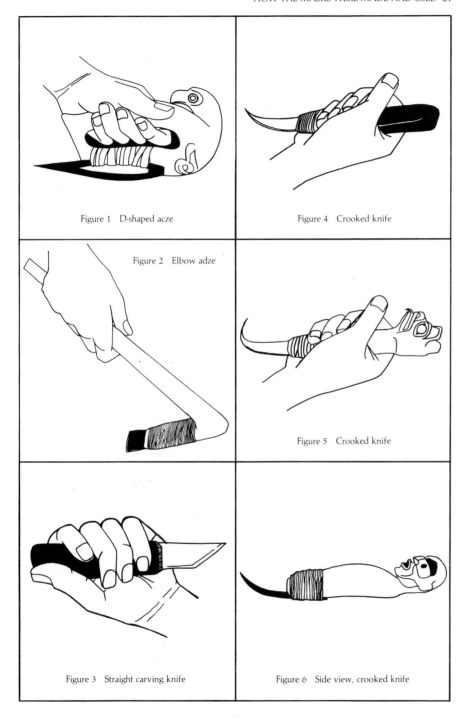

Figure 1   D-shaped acze

Figure 4   Crooked knife

Figure 2   Elbow adze

Figure 5   Crooked knife

Figure 3   Straight carving knife

Figure 6   Side view, crooked knife

depending on the carver's arm length, the power of his swing, and the volume of wood to be removed. The use of these adzes involved different motor habits from those employed with D-shaped tools. The blade and handle used by one carver might be totally unsuitable for another, so it behooved the apprentice to learn early to make the tools necessary to meet his needs. In addition the carver's personal safety had to be considered in the design and construction of tools. Experience was required to select the proper limbs from a tree for use as handles. The chosen piece must have adequate spring to it as well as proper balance. Tools must fit the carver's hands, and handles should provide an adequate grasp, insuring safety and control as he slashes at a block of wood.

A good carver was sure of each stroke. I have watched carvers with total fascination. They would swing their adzes at blocks of wood within inches of their fingertips. Yet there was never an accident.

MATERIALS

The forest surrounded every village and carving materials were there for the taking. The best and finest, as well as the most common, carving wood on the Northwest Coast was obtained from the western red cedar. In terms of quality, the best of this wood was found in the Queen Charlotte Islands. There the trees grew to enormous girth and tremendous heights, while the dense forest made for rapid vertical growth and hence minimal knots in the trunk. It was the choice wood for making the sixty-foot dugout canoes for which the Haida are justly famous.

Slimmer cedar trees grow in the upper reaches of the numerous rivers that flow westward to the coast. Red cedar becomes less common the farther north one goes into southeastern Alaska, until in the vicinity of Frederick Sound it disappears. Yellow cedar takes its place in greater abundance.

A variety of other woods were available, each with distinctive properties. Foremost was the ubiquitous alder. It seems to thrive in places where fire or timber operations have removed the conifers, and it is extremely versatile. Maple, yew, and crab apple wood were also carved, though seldom used for masks. The western red cedar and alder are the best woods for carving masks.

Cedars differ in hardness and other qualities. The dark red cedar color, for example, indicates the wood is harder than lighter red wood, so carvers chose the wood only for certain projects. Upland cedar is soft and more pliable. Both types split easily along their length. All red cedar hardens when dry and so is highly valued for making complex or mechanical masks. Finished cedar carvings could take a great deal of physical abuse with little visible damage.

Yellow cedar on the other hand is not easily split. It is coarser and more dense-grained than red cedar. Yellow cedar can, however, be used for mask carving. The Tlingit Indians availed themselves of it for the smaller shaman masks as the red cedar was not always available to them. Also red cedar can be bent wonderfully, and so it was the wood of choice for the marvelous boxes. The carver had to be careful with yellow cedar because when overly stressed it would literally explode. There is little sap in yellow cedar compared with red cedar, so the carver need take less care to avoid resin pockets.

Alder is a fine wood and was consistently used for masks. It was also selected to make ceremonial rattles incorporating intricately carved figures. Alder was used to carve oil bowls and food dishes because it imparts no odor or peculiar flavor to the food. Incidentally, weavers used the bright orange inner bark for dying woven vegetable fibre baskets. The major drawback to this wood is its marked shrinkage. Masks carved from it must be dried slowly over a long period of time lest large fractures develop across the surface. Shrinkage had to be reckoned with carefully when a carver was grappling with complex type masks.

Before proceeding to analyze some of the characteristics of masks, a definition of the mask types to be described should be made. The *single-face mask* is a representation of one face, though occasionally this face has embellishments of smaller faces and figures along the border. The *mechanical mask* is a complex one, having a single face but with movable mechanical parts attached to enhance the symbolism. The mouth, neck, eyes or arms may move or open and close while it is used. The most complex of all masks are the *transformation masks.* These are masks with one or more faces hidden behind an outer face. The outer face hides the identity of the other faces until the moment arrives for their revelation. Some masks have a combination of both mechanical and transformational characteristics. These complex masks require tremendous skill both in construction and operation.

Close examination of the Kwakiutl transformation mask illustrated (Plates 8A and 8B) and the Bella Coola mask (Plates 9A and 9B) will help the reader become more familiar with the technical problems involved in construction. The Kwakiutl mask is a family crest symbol, its outer face representing a great bullhead frog, the second face that of raven (culture hero and trickster), while the innermost mask is the ancestor. The tolerances involved in integrating all three masks presented staggering problems for the carver and can only increase our admiration and appreciation of the final result. All the woods after drying had shrunk substantial but varying amounts. Shrinkage had to be accounted for in the proper proportioning of each of the masks, so that one mask fitted snugly inside the other on completion. The outside mask was the thickest because the moving parts took the most jarring damage and stress. The face was designed to be closed crisply with a resounding snap, so the wood needed to be thick enough not to break apart. The thinnest mask was reserved for the inside face, so proportions for fitting were remarkably complicated. These factors needed to be known and carefully considered before the carver could even undertake such a project.

Yet another factor to be dealt with in carving transformation masks was the problem of weight. Too much weight or bulk would reduce the mask's effectiveness and spontaneity by inhibiting the performer's dance movements or impersonation.

In the case of the Bella Coola mask (Plate 9A) the outside face represents the salmon species, symbol of sustenance and survival. It was carved from broad-grained red cedar for the strength inherent in this wood. The inner face represents the Salmon Bringer (9B) a venerated deity who escorts the salmon in their migrations from their home at Kla'suldalalis (That Far-Away Ocean Place) to the rivers within the homeland. The inner face is carved from alder because of its light weight. Carefully dried, it can take and hold screws well for the hinged parts. The carver used four separate arms to break the outer face apart and also to equalize the distribution of weight, though these are not equal-sized parts, as the photographs reveal. Strings were attached at strategic places in the arms and outer face to open and close the mask. The placement of the strings and the movements they control are a study in their own right. It was critical for the carver to know exactly what holes were to be drilled and where they were to be located in order to avoid too much stress on the strings that activate the movable portions of the mask. Problems of stress must have kept the carver in an agitated state if he wasn't sure of himself. Not enough stress on the strings would fail to open the mask. Too much stress would result in a malfunction. The strings could snap and the mask rendered inoperative —a calamity if it occurred during a performance. (More on this mask in section on Transformation Mask.)

SPECIAL TECHNICAL CONSIDERATIONS

Whether or not mask carvers worked solely from memory prior to the coming of the Europeans in creating these faces we do not know. Certainly for the past one hundred years or more carvers have had access to materials such as paper and pencils which helped them visualize more concretely the form their work was to take. The carvers adapted to these materials with ease. In the middle 1940s I had access to a torn and fragmented ledger, the property of a Fort Rupert Kwakiutl family. It was dated around the turn of the century. This book recorded the gifts and their costs distributed to guests who had attended the lineage's potlatches. But sprinkled throughout its pages were penciled sketches of masks representing forest and sea spirits. One of the family members had recorded the faces for possible use in mask commissions. In more recent times the use of paper and pencil to sketch the technical details of a mask has become commonplace. Mungo Martin and George Nelson (Kwakiutl), and Byron Peal (Tsimshian), among others, did this as a preliminary to carving.

One of the prime secrets of the carver lay in his knowledge of the condition of the wood he was to carve. The Northwest Coast carvers never carved the intricate masks from thoroughly dried or dehydrated woods. Cedar and alder, for example, should be green and filled with moisture. The carvers worked in woods that were wringing with moisture; in some cases so green that water could be pressed out between thumb and fingers. Dry wood did not allow the carver the versatility and control—and hence the creative latitude—that moist wood permitted.

After a mask was completed, it was put away to dry slowly in some corner of the house, or in a cave or forest shelter. There was no rush to complete the masks. The carver worked slowly, methodically, with careful consideration of the nature of his materials. In a temperature between fifty and sixty degrees Fahrenheit, drying time ranged from two to four weeks, depending upon the nature of the wood. The humid climate of the coast helped in the process, as evaporation could only occur very slowly. Rapid drying would cause breaks and splits. In complex multi-faced masks, tolerances between the carved faces often amounted to less than a quarter of an inch and the carver had to be aware of varying shrinkage rates as the masks dried.

Upon completion of the drying process the mask was examined for deformation resulting from shrinkage. If it was part of a transformation mask all parts were brought together in order to determine the fit. Adjustments were made, thinning was done and edges were trimmed. If all the parts fit snugly into place they were then sanded, the remaining burrs removed, and in some cases, knife marks stippled over some surfaces for special textured effects. Painting the mask was reserved as a last step unless the mask was a mechanical type in which case the parts were painted first, then hinged together. Secondary effects were sometimes added before painting: cedar bark decoration, human hair, animal fur, or sea shells.

Kwakiutl carvers of Vancouver Island made masks with incredible ingenuity, as if they deliberately posed technical questions designed to stump their competitors (Plate 10). This is a transformation mask representing the sun as a family crest symbol. Visible are the strings coming from the eye sockets of the inner face, which connect to the inner cheeks of the outer mask. The strings come out of the cheeks to enter a hole centrally located in each of two of the four projecting appendages (Figures 16A and 16B). These appendages symbolize the sun's rays but they also have an extremely important covert function; they provide the necessary leverage for the strings by which the performer opens and closes the three separate parts of the outer face. The height of the vertical ray was calculated to provide the leverage necessary to raise the upper part of the outside face. This poses some fascinating questions about the technician. Did the mechanical need determine the outward design and style of the mask and require refashioning of traditional forms and design?

In the light of such considerations the reader is urged to examine closely the complex masks illustrated in the color section of this book as well as other transformation masks illustrated in black and white photographs.

In the case of the long, narrow masks such as the Kwakiutl Cannibal Society raven (Plate 11) and Crooked Beaks (Plates 12 and 13) additional carving problems arose. The length of these masks varies from three to six feet when completed. They may weigh from thirty to forty pounds. Lower jaws were hinged, allowing them to move and give animation to the creature. The masks were carved from large blocks of red cedar; the initial phase of such a carving operation resembled nothing so much as a wrestling match between two protagonists, the carver and the 100-pound block of wood. As much as 50% of the cedar block had to be removed in order to obtain the proper proportions of the mask. Great strength was required to get at the proper angles for adzing. In such an operation the elbow adze was the best tool. The long mask emerged from the heart wood. After the basic shape was achieved, layer after layer of cedar was stripped away with crooked knives of varying curves until the entire length of the mask had a uniform thinness. As one carver put it, "Ideally, the beak and projecting parts should be only about three-eights of an inch thick." Care was necessary all the way, lest a part be carved too thinly and thus break off. The long and slender beaks of the cannibal raven masks had to make a marvelous hollow clacking sound when the lower beak was snapped against the upper part, providing an extra aesthetic dimension for performer and audience.

The above-mentioned masks were essential in a ritual that encompassed as many as a dozen masks of similar sizes and fantastic shapes (Plates 11, 12, 14, 15). Traditional colors were red, black, and white; the heads were covered with finely shredded red cedar bark. There are many masks of this type with curved eye patterns that have been designed to catch the light from the fires when they were brought before the audiences. Eyes protruded well out of their sockets on a flat plain, giving an eerie quality to the creatures. The Kwakiutl carvers recognized these visual properties and encouraged their use to provide dramatic highlights.

STYLIZED PATTERNS AND TEMPLATES

There were certain stylized elements within the face which were common to both northern and central groups, but some tribes preferred style qualities of one type to those of another. The trained observer, however, can spot these patterns which assist in identifying tribal provenance. The elements most useful in identifying tribal preferances are the eyebrow and eye forms. The Tsimshian and Haida used eye, eyebrow, and mouth patterns that were carefully and clearly carved, being on a scale comparable to human proportions. The Kwakiutl and Bella Coola, on the other hand, preferred eye and mouth forms that were larger than life, though differences in brows are not always apparent. Also, their eye forms protruded out of the sockets more than those in the realistic

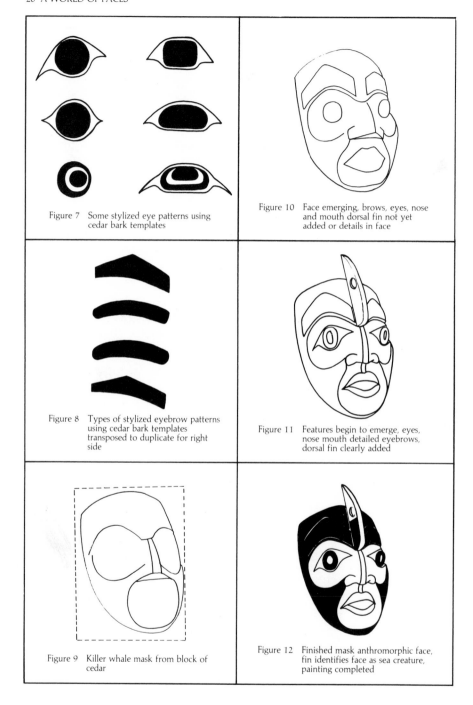

Figure 7 Some stylized eye patterns using cedar bark templates

Figure 8 Types of stylized eyebrow patterns using cedar bark templates transposed to duplicate for right side

Figure 9 Killer whale mask from block of cedar

Figure 10 Face emerging, brows, eyes, nose and mouth dorsal fin not yet added or details in face

Figure 11 Features begin to emerge, eyes, nose mouth detailed eyebrows, dorsal fin clearly added

Figure 12 Finished mask anthromorphic face, fin identifies face as sea creature, painting completed

masks of the northern peoples. Examples of eye and eyebrow patterns are seen (Figures 7 and 8).

To make the stylized features of equal size and shape for both left and right sides, the carver used templates fashioned from red cedar bark. Before cutting out these patterns the bark was thoroughly dried to prevent warping. Then, after tracing the outlines with some sort of marker in the appropriate places, so that bisymmetry was assured, the artist could continue carving.

He had to continually check his work on each side to be sure his lines and forms were not getting away from him, resulting in distortions of the face. By examining some examples in the museums, one can see that the carver did in fact lose control in some cases.

Another preference of the northern tribes was to position the eyes so that they were not cut flat against the plane of the face. Rather, the top part of the eye was cut somewhat more forward than the bottom part which in turn receded into the cheek area. Kwakiutl forms are more frequently rendered as a flat surface without the curved quality seen in the north.

SPACING AND MEASURING

Each carver had his own means for measuring distances on a wood surface. While they were primitive techniques at best, they worked marvels for the carvers. Mungo Martin and Byron Peel, as well as other carvers, measured their design surfaces with one, two, and three finger widths, making interpolations each in his own esoteric manner.

To make a mask uniformly thin and thus lightweight another trick was used. The carver thrust a short-bladed knife into the thinnest point of the face with a predetermined thickness in mind. If this section was still too thick, wood was removed until the desired thinness was reached. He would then hold the wood to the light and determine the correct thickness of the rest of the mask by comparing the quality of the light passing through the wall. The small cracks made by the blade insertions would close completely later in the drying process.

CARVING A SINGLE FACE MASK

In the old days the carver worked in seclusion, if not downright secrecy. He was spirited away by his patron to avoid contact with others who might profane his work, or he worked *incommunicado* in the patron's house, or he might secrete himself deep in a forest where few people dared venture. There were locations along the coast where dangerous spirits dwelt and hence were good places to stockpile work, if the rituals learned during an apprentice's days could mollify the spirits. The masks were usually placed in large wooden boxes and hidden in a cave or under an overhanging ledge, to thwart accidental discovery. Masks were brought to the houses in the villages when they were ready for use.

For days, or even weeks on end, the carver remained alone, in deep concentration, thinking of the form and characteristics of the faces to be carved. His first loyalty was to the crest symbols, their designs and associated forms. Meditation, prayer, and the singing of power songs that were his personal property, gave him additional encouragement.

A distinction should be made here between the masks carved by the professional for use by a patron, and the masks used by the shaman or Indian doctor to drive out or carry away the illness of a patient. Diagnostic rituals often involved the use of masks by these practitioners, especially among the northern tribes. While we know little about healers as carvers, it appears they did make their own masks as well as the other paraphernalia associated with their calling. The shaman alone knew what the faces represented, what the sources of his inspirations were, and their functions in healing. Masks of the shaman were limited to single-face types, some with multiple figures superimposed. Unfortunately we know little about them or about their carving techniques and can only speculate about the rituals in which these masks were used. Most of the masks seem to represent healers in the act of curing and singing their power songs, or spirits known intimately by the healer. There are masks that represents the souls of deceased individuals, and helpers in the healing acts. As they were made to communicate on other than social levels they remain fascinating enigmas.

When a professional carver had acquired the necessary insight, and inspiration had taken firm root, he picked up his elbow adze, a block of red cedar and began to peel away the extraneous wood. Size, shape, facial features, appendages where necessary, even surface colors and design were already firmly in his mind. The cutting away of the unneeded wood was usually done over a large log chopping block or fallen cedar log. Carvers often used their legs, knees, and thighs for additional bracing and support. The drawings that follow reveal the stages in the carving of a single face mask, in this case a representation of a killer whale man, an ancestral figure (Figures 9, 10, 11, 12). The first stage consists of defining the shape and size of the mask, bringing out the general features of the face, eyes, brows, nose, and mouth. Next the sides, top, and bottom are rounded off. When completed the carver turns the block over and begins to hollow out the inside to the proper thinness. This removal of wood accelerates the drying process. The elbow adze loosens the wood as the carver cuts away the excess amounts to within an inch of the edge. Then he uses crooked knives to clear away the loosened wood, using firm circular strokes (Figure 4).

The second stage involves the use of the crooked knives to bring out more of the detail of the face. The area around the eyes and the eye forms themselves are revealed, the brows outlined more clearly, the nose shaped as well as the nostrils. The mouth is delineated to express the appropriate emotion. A carver works by moving his knives from one generalized feature to another, never concentrating on a single feature until finished. He peels away the wood in small slivers rather than in large chunks. As one carver aptly put it, "You can always keep shaving off but once you've taken off too much wood, you can't put it back on." Carving is a process of reducing. (Figures 9 through 12).

In stage three the face emerges with greater clarity. It is at this point that the crooked knives of differing blade angles show their versatility. The roundness of the cheeks, the gentle contour of the eyes and eye details, the fullness of the lips, are brought about through the use of special curved blades. The dorsal fin which identifies the face of a killer whale is carved separately, then fitted into its position between the brows. When all the features are balanced and in proper proportion, more wood is removed from the inside to lighten it. A mask should have a uniform thinness throughout its surface, between one-fourth to one-half of an inch being ideal. The hole in the mouth is then cut through, as are the eye holes. It is fitted to the carver's face as he tries to visualize its use. Some adjustments are made in width or sides if necessary, the remaining burrs removed and smoothed. Then it is shelved for drying. (Figure 11.)

In the fourth and final stage, the mask is completed. The face surface is smoothed and sanded, and colors applied in the appropriate areas. The artist's creative imagination is exercised to the full at this stage, using decorative designs which help reveal the identity of the face. Paint brushes were made from the fur of porcupines or human hair. Painting was a slow, deliberate process. It was never hurried. Finally, if other decorative materials were to be added, such as backing, cedar bark, human hair, animal fur, or copper features, they were attached. Holes were then drilled along the edge near a point where the ears would be and a thong passed through them so the mask can be attached to the wearer's head (Figure 12).

CARVING A TRANSFORMATION MASK

In the initial stages the carving of the faces of a transformation mask followed the steps used for carving a single face. The first face (the inner face) must have those mechanical characteristics which enable it to accommodate the second mask (the outer face), integrating it harmoniously with the first.

I will use the Bella Coola mask representing the Salmon Bringer to illustrate the ingenuity of the carver as well as the complexity of design and operation required to meet the problem of revealing an idea to an audience (Plates 9A and 9B). This mask is a masterpiece of communication, bringing together the symbolism of the salmon upon which the tribes were so dependent for survival, and the magical transformation to the Being responsible for the salmon's cyclic return. The carver must have pondered at length upon the idea of transformation and lavished enormous energy in realizing its mechanical and dramatic qualities.

The foundation mask, the inside face, represents the spirit *Naokx-nim* (Naok-x [x as German *ch*] -nim), the Salmon Bringer. It was carved from alder. Its open mouth and round eyes suggest anticipation and surprise. Around the face the carver left a broad band of wood about half an inch or more in width. Into each side of this band he cut four squared notches, top, bottom, left, and right, as illustrated in (A) of Figure 13. The notches were not completely cut through, one-fourth of an inch flange was left. The notches received the four arms or appendages that would be cut and fit snugly into the notches as seen in (B). The appendages were cut from alder, after drying. The screws that would be used to attach the appendages would then hold well in it. The carver then cut three additional appendages of the same length as the first set. One end was of a width similar to the end of (B) but the other end was reduced to about half that width as seen in (C). The wider end of (C) would be hinged to the one end of (B) on each of the four arms. On these four arms the opening and closing of the transformation mask would depend.

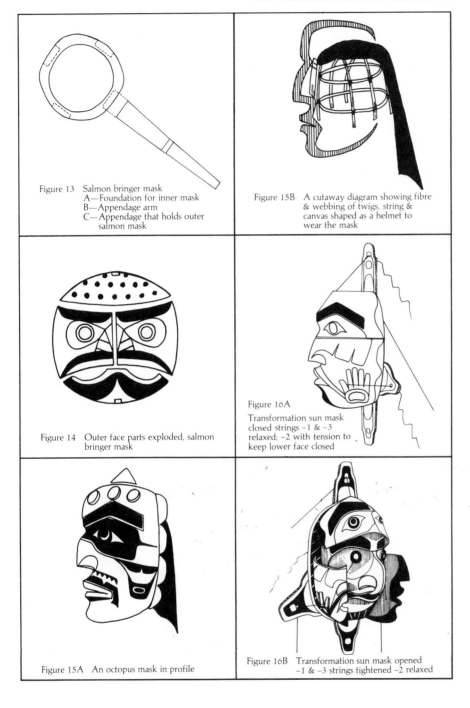

Figure 13   Salmon bringer mask
            A—Foundation for inner mask
            B—Appendage arm
            C—Appendage that holds outer
                salmon mask

Figure 15B   A cutaway diagram showing fibre
              & webbing of twigs, string &
              canvas shaped as a helmet to
              wear the mask

Figure 14   Outer face parts exploded, salmon
            bringer mask

Figure 16A

Transformation sun mask
closed strings –1 & –3
relaxed; –2 with tension to
keep lower face closed

Figure 15A   An octopus mask in profile

Figure 16B   Transformation sun mask opened
              –1 & –3 strings tightened –2 relaxed

A major technical problem is encountered with the outside face which represents a salmon's head. (Figure 14.) It is carved of red cedar, but in four separate parts. The salmon jaw is separately carved (D) as is the part which fits the topmost arm, representing the salmon's forehead (E). The two central parts from brow to upper lip are carved in two symmetrical pieces separately (F). The carver continually switched from one side of the face to the other to keep both similar in expression. The most critical of problems besetting the carver lay with the proper angles of the fitting edges. They had to be of a uniform thinness but not so thin as to run the risk of the face snapping in two. All parts had to be fitted over the inner face to assure clearance. The eyes must be of uniform size and placement so one did not droop below the other; the nose and nostrils must be equally balanced, and the lips come together without either sagging.

When the parts had been completed the carver hollowed the inside and fit them over the outer face. At this time it was imperative he keep in mind the shrinkage factors both for the red cedar and the alder parts. If he trimmed too much the outer face would be too small to fit over the inner face. One part might imbalance the other if he did not leave adequate space for trimming after the drying was completed.

The final stage of carving remained. He cut out four effigies of salmon in profile, leaving the bottom sides flat. He added these both for symbolic value and to serve as a decorative device for each of the four arms. He undoubtedly experienced deeply religious communion as he felt the Salmon Bringer's presence, or contemplated with awe the wonder of the endless return of these marvelous creatures. The four salmon symbolized the species that flooded the rivers of the Bella Coola in their respective seasons, enriching all the people.

All the loose parts were brought together and the fitting determined. The technical problems had been anticipated and trimming was now done to provide a good fit. Drying of all the parts followed. The outside face parts were notched to accept the appendages that moved the mask. The two appendages reserved for each of the four sides were then hinged together, the screws holding well in the dried and hardened alder. Care had to be taken with the angles so that in opening and closing the mask came together as one face. All the parts were sanded and the surface painted. The symbolism used in the painting and decorating was a special part of the artist's freedom and will be discussed below.

The one remaining test to be overcome, and not the least of the series of tests faced by the carver, was the technical problem of opening and closing the mask through the use of strings. The carver had constructed the mouth and jaw of the outside face so that they could be dropped by simply releasing the string attached to that part with a stop which determined the amount of the drop. The upper part of the outside face was opened by lifting it with a string that runs from the bottom of the appendage (near the fish effigy's tail) to the top of the fish head. The height of the rise could be controlled by the string. A staggering problem—the biggest of all, in fact—involved the two side or cheek parts. The carver solved this problem in the following way.

He connected string of great durability from a point behind the tail of each of the two horizontal salmon effigies, running it through a hole made in the two appendages, then drilled two additional holes to the immediate left of the one appendage and to the right of the other appendage, and ran the strings through them. The carver knew he had to get the strings to the far sides of each appendage to gain the leverage necessary to pull the outer mask closed. By releasing all the strings except the top (and pulling on that one) he was able to thrust open all the parts of the face with an explosive vigor, revealing the inner face of the Salmon Bringer. In the semi-darkness of firelight with its muted flames and dancing shadows, this must have made a spectacle to remember!

The carver had more freedom in painting the surface designs than in carving the sculptural form. Note the inside of the outer face. The paint is reddish in color and the design is formed into squares of uniform size. They may represent salmon flesh. The lines in black of varied thinness and width, in horizontal and vertical directions, represent the fish weirs in which the migrating salmon were caught. The numerous black dots covering the forehead symbolize the physiological change salmon undergo prior to spawning. In all, it is an extraordinary mask comprehending all the lore associated with the fish and its profound significance to the tribe.

It is interesting to speculate about the unknown carver and his mask. That he was an artist with vision there can be little doubt. He took profound pains with the inner face and totally captured its spiritual content. He seemed to have lavished love and care on it. But the outer face is another matter. It seems as though he was hurried with it and possibly even rough in handling it. Perhaps he was running out of time, or his patience had been taxed to the fullest by the technical problems involved. As he seemed determined to finish, he may have made his finest statement with the inner mask and then became bored with the outer face. Perhaps the outer face had less significance than the inner one. We shall never know.

THE OPERATION OF MASKS

The carver conceived, designed, and worked out the problems inherent in operating the masks. Single face masks depended upon the actor's general mien and gesture before the audience for their impact in presentation. But mechanical and transformational masks involved many other considerations. The performer wearing a complex mask had to know all the nuances of operation. There could be no flaw in his performance. Too much family prestige and tribal status was involved to take a chance on anything less than perfection.

The patron of a commissioned mask seldom if ever wore it before his guests. In most cases someone of proper position and status from his kinsmen's group was delegated the job so that the mask was not demeaned. The impersonator was responsible for learning the intimate workings of the complex mask and had to have the mask adjusted to his head and body so it did not sag while in operation. He had to know the dance steps and movements of the performance perfectly, the exact timing for his entry, synchronized with the songs and staccato beats of the drums. He had to be able to simulate the creature so that it was believable, as a giant octopus, a supernatural eagle, a wild man of the forests, or a revered ancestor spirit. Further, he had to move to different parts of the house with the proper turns around the fire, first to the sections where the chiefs and leading tribesmen were seated, and last of all to the area near the door where commoners sat. Rehearsals were therefore necessary.

Rehearsals were usually held in places remote from the village where others would least suspect something of this nature was taking place. Sometimes rehearsals would be held where the masks were hidden, sometimes closer to the village for easier access. In rehearsals the performer learned to operate the mask. He had to be able to distinguish between the numerous strings he held in his hands: which to pull to open, which to pull to close, which are relaxed, which are held rigid for the proper synchronized effects (Figures 16A and 16B).

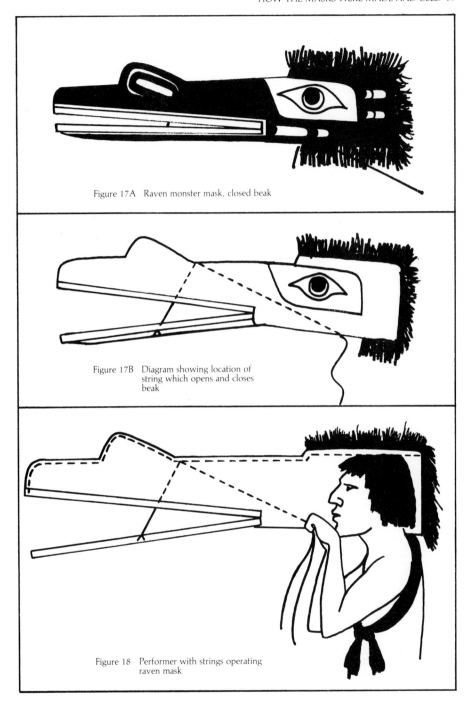

Figure 17A Raven monster mask, closed beak

Figure 17B Diagram showing location of
string which opens and closes
beak

Figure 18 Performer with strings operating
raven mask

During the last days of rehearsals, strings were carefully checked again and again for frayed edges, or for any evidence of having been tampered with by rivals who would like nothing better than to have seen the masks malfunction and therefore become a source of embarrassment to the host.

In rehearsals the patron gave instruction in the proper procedures; patron and carver watched the effects with critical eyes. Does the mask close well? Does it look convincing? Will the moment of surprise come off perfectly? Will it be the marvel he had hoped for? The fear of a falter, a mishap, or an accident in the mask's operation was like a dagger poised at the heart of the anxious patron. If the performance came off flawlessly the pressure was relieved, a crisis diffused, a sigh of relief came like a breath of fresh air from performer, kinsmen, patron, and not least, the carver himself.

Masks are held securely on the heads of impersonators by a variety of methods. The simplest is a strong cord attached to the back of a small and lightweight face. Masks somewhat bulkier in size and with more weight may require a series of cords or belts made from hide that fasten the mask securely.

Larger than life masks may be secured by a webbing used (Figure 15B) for the Kwakiutl octopus mask. It is made from bent twigs and held together by commercial twine or fish line. Part of this webbing is nailed to the mask's inner face and acts as a harness. It fits over the entire head of the wearer. Animal fur, shredded cedar bark, or trade cloth often top the webbing to hide the back of the head.

Large masks like the Crooked Beaks, Cannibal Ravens, and Cannibal Monster masks (Plates 11, 12, 13, 14) as well as the transformation types, were often too heavy to be secured around the performer's head. He had to be harnessed into them using tethers made from animal hide or twisted cedar bark ropes. These were secured to the base of the mask then tied around the performer's shoulders and across his chest (Figures 17A, 17B, 18). The large heavy masks of forty pounds or more required two sets of ropes to insure against accidents. Performers actually danced with these large burdens. Their movements were strong, controlled, and active. I have seen them.

On the other hand, the performer's vision was limited in such large masks, so guidance was required if he was to move about correctly. Attendants were designated to guide him into the dancing area and to assist him while executing the complex dance steps. When the dance was completed they also guided the performer out of the house and assisted in loosening the harness.

SPECIAL EFFECTS

In any of these complex and varied masked performances there were many special effects. Most important was the costume associated with the special spirit or Being, a garment of eagle feathers for the Kwikwis or Sea Eagle (Plate 1) or dyed cedar bark covering (Plate 14).

Almost all of the dances were accompanied by a chorus of singers who sang the songs associated with the mask. Songs were considered a type of intangible property belonging to the host or patron. The drum beats, the stylized speeches used by the leaders in setting the scene for the masked performers' entry, were important elements also requiring familiarity and rehearsal on the part of participants.

Little known, though of no less importance, were the "voices" of the Beings represented by the masks and the songs. Each tribe associated distinct voices with each spirit or supernatural being in the drama. There were many kinds of whistles used in the winter dances, whistles of different shapes, sizes, and sounds. These would be sounded in the deep forests during the preparation for the dances, strange, eerie, forbidding sounds, particularly to the ininitiated—those lacking familiarity with these particular spirits. Each whistle or voice represented the cry of the Being or creature that was to appear in the dances; each was used in a specific way and no other. For example, the whistle of the great horned owl was used during potlatches only when a chief was about to break a copper (a symbol of great wealth) before a rival from another tribe.

The art of the mask maker was at the heart of these great performances, enhancing and enriching every other element in them, indispensable in portraying the impressive personae of the mythic world and in projecting its total drama and power to the audience.

CHAPTER III

MOTIVATIONS FOR MASK MAKING

The earliest European explorers have left their impressions of the masks and their usage among the Northwest Coast Indians. Since the art was well developed by then, we can assume that masks had been produced for a very long time. So when we speak of their beginnings we are peering back into prehistory, and there are no records to help us.

The needs of the tribes differed little from the needs of other tribal groups found throughout the world. It is their distinctive responses to those needs, i.e. their rituals, their arts, that arrest our admiration and attention.

Their region no doubt also had its effect upon their arts. On the coastal strip they found themselves in a world of ocean, shore, forests, and to their east, mountains. Within their long, narrow land life took a multitude of forms. Both land and sea abounded with creatures seemingly infinitely varied; in the sea, huge whales and (so-called) killer whales, powerful sea lions, dangerous sharks; in the forests, wolves, black and grizzly bears, moose, deer, mink, ferrets; in the high country, mountain sheep and mountain goats. Each creature was seen to have endowments that were admired and had to be reckoned with. Yet things were not always what they appeared to be. Bears, when mortally wounded, sound strangely human in their suffering. In other creatures there were glimpses of a shape, a manner or stance, a voice, suggesting some affinity with human beings. These people saw all creatures as endowed with a spirit, a vital force, which gave them their existence. Magical qualities were all-pervading and all things were possible if conditions were right.

Try to picture this world of primeval man on the Northwest Coast. Always green, seasonally lush, the region was also a dark and brooding place during winter months and early spring. Yet in the late spring and summer the sea and land vibrated with life of all kinds; the days were filled with sunlight; the ocean was gentle and serene. But it could also be a frightening adversary. With little warning it might explode into storms, unleashing a fury to fill veteran seafarers with terror. In winter, heavy mantles of fog and clouds could blur the vision; islands literally disappeared from sight with the changing action of the tides; then just as suddenly reappeared. At low tides another world of pulsating life was revealed on the wet sands and in the rocky pools. The forests were to be avoided. Though known to be filled with countless creatures, they could be bafflingly silent—and then come to life for no apparent reason, creaking and groaning with mysterious sounds. Winters were cold, frost lines crisply etched across the forested slopes. The wind was biting.

To the gifted peoples of this region, the spirits of the creatures with whom they shared the land, and the phenomena of nature, benign or hostile, familiar yet ultimately mysterious, seemed to demand images which would capture the attributes, otherwise almost ungraspable, of these beings or forces. Something that would, in effect, personify them. Masks were carved to represent the spirit of night, of winter, of cold, of the south wind which brings the storms. Since all human beings in that culture had their counterparts, artists might depict them as salmon people, mosquito people, and countless others. Nothing in this world escaped the close attention of the carvers who saw everything with a face, even lowly creatures such as sea urchins or kelp. The personification of this myriad world through masks in some sense explained the unknown and assuaged fears of it.

Could the spiritual forces that were everywhere in nature be contained? The people saw themselves as vulnerable to powerful supernatural beings who were known to reside near them. To communicate with this multitude of spirits was a necessity. If the powers could be persuaded to remain neutral or to intercede on the people's behalf during crisis periods, a measure of security might be achieved. Masks which symbolized such forces were created and became a part of complex religious rituals designed to provide harmony between spirits and man.

The basic, continuing need for food also led to mask making. One could never be certain that the abundance of food would remain. Would the salmon come again? If the spirits of the salmon were appeased and treated with consideration, surely they would return to the shores. Salmon were thought to be much like human beings but living in a water habitat. They would hear the songs, the pleas to return, and changing to their fish forms they would come back each year if the propitiation was done properly.

All human beings seem to need the psychological security of knowing their roots. For the Northwest Coast Indians, it was of primary importance to know one's ancestors, and to provide public recognition and honor for them. To these people the past was rich, venerable, and filled with awesome events which must always be remembered. The past also provided the customs that taught valuable lessons for surviving. People felt it was necessary to expound on their origins, to tell others of the accomplishments of their families' past—from ancient mythological times to the present. These lineage histories had a sanctity of their own. In order to recall them and enable descendants to visualize them, masks were carved. The faces fulfilled the needs for identity and continuity. The reenactments of these momentous events in dramatic form brought the people a sense of pride in the past and of accomplishment in the present. The masks representing ancestors were symbols of the veracity of their roots.

There were needs for assurance against other uncertainties, accidents, illness, even death. Where does illness come from? What can man do to cope with these problems? Where does he go after death? The tribes believed that in the body of each person dwelt multiple souls, and if these could be lured away from the body illness would result. How can this be prevented from happening? If the soul travels when it leaves the body, where does it go? To other spirit worlds that existed simultaneously with the daily world man occupies? These questions were no less vital than those dealing with food, shelter, and protection from spirit powers. As in other cultures, rituals evolved which addressed these most profound of all questions. Perhaps the rituals arose from mere customs or formulae that seemed to produce results and so were shared and repeated. When the same routines were repeated regularly they provided a sense of security and eventually became enshrined as formal rituals which were enriched as the society developed, with songs, dances, masks. In some cases these became very complicated because they served multiple needs. The continuous repetition of rituals, generation after generation, endowed them with sanctity. Rituals were affirmations of faith, rooted in tradition, giving people a sense of security and well-being. Masks were carved which would allay fears, would serve to provide assurances, and depict spirits as protectors, benefactors, or helpers.

The need for recognition and self-expression was inherent in the culture of the Northwest Coast Indians. The desire to be honored for accomplishments and to acquire prestige and the admiration of others was acutely felt by the tribes. Their cultural foundations were predicated on the assumption that there were stations in life. In a very real sense, status needs were answered by the acquisition of extraordinary possessions. Masks were one such possession, and people were strongly motivated to acquire them.

Masks also represented supernatural beings who were encountered by a revered ancestor. As advertisements of such unusual meetings, they became much coveted forms of wealth and in some areas of the Northwest Coast masks were eagerly negotiated for as part of a marriage dowry. They were indeed valuable property, and showing them to others under prescribed circumstances brought the owner much honor.

There was the need to display ownership of these masks for the stories they told about a lineage's past. Indian carvers were encouraged to create visual forms which could be used to fulfill such needs.

MASKS AS SYMBOLS

There are innumerable variations of Northwest Coast mask styles and types, and more variations within each of these. But most of them deal with incidents in lineage and clan histories. Animals and birds symbolized crests belonging to tribal divisions, but as styles and imagery proliferated and were embroidered, overlap with the stories of other groups would occur. No one family or tribal group owned one crest or mask type exclusively; other groups owned like stories (though with some alteration in plot or characters); stories also might be acquired by families through episodes which the ancestors of both shared—and sometimes there was outright copying. The tribes continuously innovated, inventing novel departures from the main themes—and there was always a great deal of borrowing.

All the tribal groups of the Northwest Coast shared a general belief in a primeval condition in the most remote time—long before the appearance of the world as they knew it—the mythic world of the very distant past. It was the time when all the world's living creatures came into existence and momentous human events followed. Descriptions of this world suggest a combination of our Garden of Eden and Golden Age. Animals, birds, sea creatures, and human beings gradually appeared on earth, sharing several different types of environment which no longer exist. Mankind was not above these other creatures but rather occupied a position roughly equal to them or in some cases, beneath them. But all had powers enabling them to transform themselves from one outward form to another, since external coverings were the only differences between them. They could discard their skins, feathers, or fur and assume different forms, yet they spoke a common language. It is essential for the reader to accept this viewpoint in order to understand the nature of the world the masks represent. It was a world far too rich, too complex, too mysterious to *depict*. But it could be powerfully *symbolized* in the masks; and the master carvers knew well how to do this with a maximum of emotional intensity.

Within this marvelous mythic world there were four physical divisions where living creatures dwelt. One was the earth realm which was inhabited by the myth people, those animals, birds, sea creatures, and human beings who became the ancestors of the tribes; eagles, raven, wolves, killer whales, grizzly bear, and so on.

There was the world of spirits and ghosts which some thought of as residing in an underworld. Inhabitants lived in ways similar to those on earth except their day was night, their winter summer, and so on. They were human-like beings, but they lacked substance. They could be dangerous and were avoided whenever possible.

There was the undersea realm where different kinds of supernatural beings resided, not just the salmon and other fish, but fantastic creatures such as the giant octopus. Known as Komokwa to the Kwakiutl, the octopus ruled over a watery kingdom which included the seals, whales, loon, sea gulls, even sea anemones as his subjects. In the sea there lived other monsters in the form of whales and killer whales, sea wolves, sea eagles—all kinds of fantastic creatures. Each was endowed with various powers beyond ordinary creatures.

The fourth realm was the sky world where enormous birds lived, those that acted as guardians of the sun, or sky eagles, thunderbirds, and among one particular tribe, the habitat of the Supreme Being who created the world.

Miraculous events took place in each of these realms and the people's oral literature records countless episodes, most of which made contact with the daily lives of the Indians in one way or another. This compelling mythic world was both dramatic and convincing; the belief that it once existed continues to have a hold on some of these people to the present day.

There were special beings who had lived in that Golden Age, who had to be remembered—the culture heros of the tribes. Though not always human, they could take human form. They had been responsible for shaping the world the Indians knew. Each region of the Northwest Coast—north, central, south—had its heroes. There were wonderful stories told about their exploits; those who brought the sun to its present place in the sky, or who released the moon and stars that provided light in the darkness of night. Momentous events in that mythic world made possible the movement of the tides enabling future occupants of the earth realm to garner food more easily. Heroes created the streams and rivers where the salmon would spawn; revealed the islands off the coast; molded the mountains. Some heros gave animals and birds their respective names, coloration, cries or voices, habits, and idiosyncrasies. There was no end to what they could do! Some heroes answered to a multitude of names. They established illustrious lineages and clans which exist today. Raven of the North, creator of the Haida, Tlingit, and Tsimshian tribes, was one such hero. To the Bella Coola, he was the founder of their arts and the Creator's right hand man. A Tlingit once said to me, "To understand us, you must know our myths, our stories."

An episode from the mythic age serves as an example. The southern Kwakiutl tribes describe a cave which once became a source of supernatural treasures for an ancestress. It is called Nawala-gwatzi, "the receptacle of magic." A lady had once been kind to a lowly creature, and in return she was told the whereabouts of a cave where forest dwellers met to socialize. Secretly, she watched them assemble and take off their garments and masks. The animals were grouse, wolf, kingfisher, weasel, frog, deer, and others. All assumed human forms before her eyes. They proceeded to dance together. When it was discovered that a human being was watching them they were dismayed. To secure her silence as to the whereabouts of the cave, the animals gave her the rights to use their masks for dances. These masks became her lineage's property and were considered treasures. Many lineages share such a myth though the characters vary from group to group. This is an instance of a revelation in which animals had human counterparts, and masks served as reminders of such events.

Each lineage or clan had a multitude of myths which explained the many sides of ancestral exploits. These frequently took the form of personal encounters with spirits. When this happened, a man emerged, transformed by self-awareness, with the assurances from a benefactor that he would be helped through life.

Since masks were gifts bestowed on ancestors by supernatural beings, they became symbols of history. They were carved according to the instructions given about them, including their songs, dance steps, even care in storage. They were spiritual as well as material possessions. As one Tlingit woman put it in 1965, "Masks—and clan hats—are our shrines."

The tribal carvers were given the responsibility for capturing the essense of such encounters and portraying the characters involved in these myriad incidents. There were ancestors who came from the sky world, descending on a copper ladder or even copper totem poles; others portray thunderbirds or eagles who settled on the earth, even eagles who resided on the bottom of the sea. They took off their garments and masks, transforming themselves into real people. An ancestor descended from the sky in the form of a grizzly bear; another arrived wearing a face representing the sun. Sea spirits gave ancestors rights to use masks which represented whales, killer whales, even the fearsome octopus. A forest spirit bestowed the gift of a nightmare-bringer in order to intimidate enemies. Wolves bestowed on an ancestor certain masks representing the spirits of ghost people, and enabled their owner thereafter to protect himself from such beings. Examples of this nature could be cited endlessly.

All gifts of this sort provided the people with assurances as well as a sense of pride and prestige. Masks represented truths about the nature of man and the place he occupied within the order of things. Inherent in the power of the masks was the full recognition of their symbolism and a firm belief in their efficacy. The very existence of the masks seemed to verify the events they symbolized.

THE ROLES MASKS PLAY

Tribes on the Northwest Coast did not always share the same visions or have the same myths or heroes. They differed somewhat also in their use of masks, though there were also shared motivations and uses. For example, all of them used masks in highly theatrical performances. (Sometimes there were very private ceremonies which also made use of masks.) In all tribes masks served a number of functions but in none were they created by the carvers to meet purely *aesthetic* needs. The carver conceived the forms to serve *human* needs. The masks were vehicles of communication; they were reminders of the people's roots. They were the books of a culture which did not have a written language to record important events. Some embodied the wisdom of the past, as discussed above, and served to enshrine hallowed episodes in the mind's eye. What they symbolized was important; it had to be remembered.

Masks were intended to be worn but not everyone had the right to wear one or to impersonate the spirit that was represented. That could prove dangerous. With the exception of some purely social kind of masks and those used by medicine men for healing, the use of masks in ceremonies was usually restricted to the fall and winter months. This period was considered the sacred time of the year, when the spirits which dwelt among the people were close at hand. Men could commune with them. Masks were brought out for the major rituals and social events called potlatches, i.e. great feasts of an intertribal or interclan nature. But a lineage or clan did not present masked performances every year and only certain highly-placed families aspired to give potlatches in which their valued possessions, the masks, were brought before the guests as part of a formalized presentation. Only specifically designated individuals representing a host or patron had the power necessary to hold or wear them; kinsmen helped enact complicated rituals for presentation before guests. Once the masks were revealed to the public, custom required that the host distribute wealth to the people. In effect, invited guests were paid to witness such performances. Expenditure of huge amounts of wealth were expected of those who brought out their masks in public and who discussed their symbolism and meaning before others.

Invitations were extended to guests a year or two in advance of such proceedings. As host, a chief and his family expected to provide food, comforts, entertainment, and gifts for guests who sometimes numbered in the hundreds. Since there were scores of lineages and clan groupings, there were only a few potlatches at any one time in any given year.

A chief or patron exhibited his masks and the prerogatives which accompanied them during such ceremonies. When the masks were not in use they were carefully stored in the homes of the chiefs. These men served as the custodians of lineage and clan possessions. Custom differed from region to region, however, on whether the masks could be disposed of or whether they were sacrosant. This question became critical in the tribal responses to alien pressures of the middle and late nineteenth century. It will be discussed further in Chapter V.

Masks were never worn in daily social intercourse; no one wore them except in their proper contexts, save for masks employed, only rarely, for fun events (Plate 34). Rituals were highly charged visual and emotional events, in which musical instruments, flutes, rattles, box or log drums, and a chorus of singers were used. Body postures, symbolic gestures, dance steps, and special costumes were aspects of each masked performance. Each mask had a name, a special facial characteristic, colors, surface designs or patterns, all of which helped reveal the identity of the spirit or being which was impersonated. The length of time that masks were worn varied with the ceremonies. Some were used for not more than a few seconds, then vanished from sight. Other masks were worn for as much as twenty or thirty minutes during complicated stories. Each chieftain who potlatched controlled the rights to a score or more of masks. Exhibiting them in the context of a myth narrative accompanied by dance and pantomine could take several hours.

Masks were never held loosely in the hands and they were never treated casually or disrespectfully. They were not placed on walls in exhibit fashion, as we do. After use they were carefully placed in storage boxes within the home, hidden from the eyes of outsiders. They might not be used again for a dozen or more years, but they would be used again. The present owner might not live to present them himself but whoever inherited them would. Masks were considered special property. They were carefully guarded against loss of any kind. The clan heads had always been held responsible for their safety, but this attitude changed drastically under white impact and missionary influ- ence, and the masks began to diminish among the numerous tribes of the Northwest Coast about the 1880s. Some groups resisted for years, however, rallying around the symbolism of the masks and what they represented, refusing to give them up.

A particularly interesting use of ritual masks is found in the secret societies associated with the Tsimshian, northern Kwakiutl, Bella Coola, and southern Kwakiutl tribal divisions. Membership in such organizations cut across clan or lineage lines making many people eligible to join them. Ceremonies were centered around winter activities and were strong unifying forces within the tribe. A proliferation of orders and sub-orders of these societies developed, each with masks associated with special uses and kinds of performance. There were healing societies made up of shaman, there were conjuring societies, war societies, and societies for inducting young people or adults as new members. The initiates in all secret societies were induced into trance-like states for communion with spirits, some of which were terrifying. In each of these secret societies there were characteristics that were both entertaining and frightening. They involved wild men, voracious women, cannibal spirits, whales who lived on the sun, thunderbirds, and serpents with double faces, to name just a few. Journeys to the undersea or to the sky worlds were prominent in the dramas, each place visualized as being inhabited by fantastic beings. Some had long fierce countenances, repulsive habits, the more to terrorize and intimidate the uninitiated.

While space does not permit descriptions of the winter dances of all these tribes, the southern Kwakiutl will serve as example of these cere-monies. Their winter dances were called Tse-Tse-qa, the secrets. A coveted membership was that of the cannibal society ritual in which a bewildering variety of large masked figures participated, some exceeding five feet in length. Another series of secret society performances (which incidentally were held in public) were referred to as ghost power dances. Performances demonstrated the acquisition of gifts from the ghost people. A third were war dances, revealing the power resulting from invincibility in war or invulnerability to pain, or the power to throw diseases into enemies, as well as the power to conjure spirits into visible form, which enabled the conjurer to demonstrate his control over these spirits (Toog-wid).

There were many masked performances associated with the serious side of religious beliefs and other rituals. There were exceptions. One was secular entertainment. Another was the shamanistic or curing rites performed by healing specialists.

Among the southern Kwakiutl, the people gathered in villages fol-lowing the conclusion of salmon fishing activities. Spontaneous dances included the lighthearted use of masks just for fun. These informal gatherings were called gwom-yasa or play potlatching. In an outburst of mimicry and humor, people were presented in caricature and individual idiosyncracies trumpeted. Kinsmen were depicted regardless of position or station in life, whether man, woman, or child. Individuals were likened to animals or fish or other creatures, providing comic relief and evoking spasms of laughter. Much of this mirth was scatalogical. Masks were crudely carved and poorly finished, often being discarded after use. A few of these have found their way into private collections and are more valuable for their ethnological than their aesthetic significance. Their purpose did not require great skill. They were made by ordinary people to serve momentary ends.

An exception of far greater significance were those masks that belonged to the shaman, the specialists involved in the arts of healing the sick. Shaman or Indian doctors cured illness, and maintained the equilibrium of the tribe in times of acute crisis. Their knowledge of the spirit world and their skills in communicating with dwellers of that realm were considerable. They were able through their esoteric knowledge to manipulate the spirits and often controlled their actions.

There resided in each village a shaman or two, each a specialist of a sort. All of them were supposed to know how to protect the people from the evils of sorcery and witchcraft, always a threat to peace and security. The shaman communicated with all kinds of spirits and supernatural beings and often restored a person to health through the use of this power. The shaman retrieved straying souls which had wandered from a person's body. They drove out intrusive substances which often caused temporary illnesses (Plates 48, 49, 50, 51).

Each shaman's paraphernelia included masks which he used to cure, an activity that was not, of course, confined to any specific time of the year. Each shaman had his own curing techniques, rituals, masks, even songs that helped to heal. There were occasionally female shamans. The masks often portrayed special beings, sometimes known as helpers, in the healing arts. A practitioner did not supplicate these spirits; he acted on his own will, compelling all intruding forces to do his bidding. Shaman were given a great deal of respect by the populace, in some ways being apart from the group.

No two shaman used the same masks because their powers differed. They appeared to have carved their own rather than hiring a carver specialist to create the mask for them. Not very much is known about their uses and meaning. For the shaman to disclose the nature and source of his healing powers would be a fatal transgression. His control over the spirits would evaporate and he would probably perish. Such disclosure might also create havoc for the people. Tlingit, Haida, and Tsimshian tribal groups commonly employed the masked shaman for healing rituals, but among the Kwakiutl and Bella Coola tribes this practice was less developed and given minor public exposure.

CHAPTER IV

MASKS AS A FORM OF COMMUNICATION

A long the length of the coast masks served the same purposes and performed the same functions. These functions were threefold: first, masks used in tribal ceremonies to contact, propitiate, and celebrate the invisible world; secondly, masks to represent ancestors' origins and achievements; and lastly, masks used by shaman in contacting the spirit world in order to cope with disease, misfortune, and other personal or tribal crisis. There can be little doubt that some tribes influenced neighbors, the ideas of one group being adapted by others nearby. The Bella Coola tribes acknowledged artistic and cultural debts to the southern Kwakiutl, the Haida to the northern Kwakiutl, Nootkans to southern Kwakiutl, and Tlingit to Tsimshian, who, incidentally, were enormously admired.

A number of regional mask styles developed from north to south, each with distinctive preferences and characteristics. One fact must be kept in mind: while a summary of mask styles may serve as a general guide, it is at best an oversimplification because mask making was a complex, extensively employed, and deeply entrenched practice. Three classes of masks may be discerned in each of these tribal regions. There were the intra-tribal masks which were expressive of local recognition and use and were not acknowledged or accepted outside that group. There were the inter-tribal masks whose symbolism and characteristics were used and recognized between tribes of similar cultural and linguistic backgrounds. These were often used in rituals and ceremonies in which the spectators were outsiders, even competitors but who also shared, in general, the way of life and values of the host tribe. The third class of masks were of an esoteric nature, being employed by the shaman for healing. For the most part shaman masks were restricted to use within the tribe itself, but there were occasional exceptions to the

rule. Shaman masks were distinctive because there was little communication between the practitioner and the spectators, a characteristic not
lacking with inter- and intra-tribal mask use. The shaman worked alone,
his actions, incantations, seances, and gestures being little understood or
recognized by the patient or his family who often stood close by and
watched.

The human face was probably the single most common mask representation. It is remarkably adaptive in form and plasticity and capable of
assuming many expressions. There is a great range of emotional content
which can be captured in the human face and the carvers of the Northwest were gifted in depicting expressive facial conformations. Equally
important were the faces of animals and birds and the familiar supernatural beings; eagle, grizzlies, wolves, ravens, and so on. The carver
used the mask as a vehicle for integrating the human face with other
living creatures around them.

Faces had separate and distinctive parts whether they represented
animals, birds, or human beings. These parts were formalized eyebrows,
eyes of varying shapes and sizes, nose, and mouth. Each feature was
sharply defined and precisely drawn. They were further defined through
the application of paint often in bold colors, preferably black, red, or
turquoise blue. Painted designs were often added, providing additional
means by which characters could be identified.

THE NORTHERN MASKS

The Tlingit, Haida, and Tsimshian tribes shared many mask characteristics in common, and the carvers probably moved from one to another
in the past. I would hesitate to identify unequivocally some masks as
being from one group rather than another, unless there were accompanying documentation. Northern masks are generally smaller in size
than those of the central region. They used paint more sparingly also,
leaving more wood surfaces exposed.

A significant proportion of the masks are portrait-type faces, realisti-
cally carved to represent actual people. Other humanoid masks represented animals and birds of benign, even charming facial expressions.
The face masks were carved in meticulous detail with realism a funda-
mental characteristic. The facial parts follow real-life faces with skin-like
surfaces seemingly stretched tautly over bone foundations (Plates 41,
42, 46). Northern masks were superbly sensitive as portraits and very

believable. Using restraint in paint, small touches of designs were often applied to forehead, nose, or cheek regions. Compressed within tiny spaces, these designs nevertheless were deceptively free in form though complex in patterns. If removed from the mask itself the design could stand on its own as an interesting entity. Designs also served as helpful clues in identifying the character of the mask (Plates 17, 20, 22, 26B). These masks were inter-tribal in nature, being used as sources of communication between the various tribal divisions of the north.

The Tsimshian masks were sensitive renderings of human portrayals and are considered among the finest masterpieces of the Northwest Coast. Commemorative in nature, they are eloquent examples of the carver's skills. Representing recently deceased people they were exhibited intra-tribally during memorial potlatch services (Plates 41 and 52).

Generally speaking, the northern masks were less complex in construction than those found in the central region. Mechanical masks were not commonly employed, but some are extant. They have strong emotional appeal because they are so human, their appeal being heightened by some mechanical parts that were built into the faces; mouths and eyes that open and close, eyebrows that rise and descend. These features were manipulated by the impersonator with strings hidden within the mask (Plates 2, 3, 53 and 56). Movable faces gave an illusion of life, bringing surprise and delight to the audience.

It is not always possible to distinguish between masks used in intra-tribal or inter-tribal ceremonies and those used exclusively in shaman curing rites. The commonest shaman mask, however, is a single face of simple lines or those with some clusters of minor faces sculptured into cheek or forehead areas. Masks used by the healers are elusive and difficult to interpret because there is so little information about them. Shaman masks in various museum collections were in fact salvaged by collectors trespassing on grave sites where practitioners were buried. Their healing objects were left by the natives with the bodies out of a fear of contamination or illness. It is difficult to visualize a practicing shaman giving away his masks whether for personal gain or for any other reason. As individuals, they were among the most secret and conservative of people.

A large percentage of shaman masks lack eye holes while others have such tiny apertures as to seem hardly adequate for any vision. Perhaps all that was needed was the internal vision. Shaman masks were commonly used among Tlingit, Haida, and Tsimshian practitioners, hardly ever among the tribes of the central region.

CENTRAL COAST MASKS

The numerous southern Kwakiutl tribes and the Bella Coola employed countless numbers of masks in their intra- and inter-tribal potlatches, secret society rites and initiations, comedy and theatrical activities. Both tribal groups employed a wide range of types from the elementary human face with a minimum of facial details to larger-than-life faces surrounded by halos of smaller faces and figures. More popular still were ceremonial masks with infinite numbers of appendages, movable parts, faces within faces. There were masks that gyrated, rotated, or popped up from secret places within the larger mask.

In the middle and latter part of the nineteenth century the naturalistic faces grew bolder and mechanically more complex, reaching a height of development in the transformation mask. Used in inter-tribal dramas, particularly as crest symbols to impress invited guests of other tribes, the transformation mask brought a miraculous surprise, a sense of awe and respect, and at times downright shock. The Kwakiutl were acknowledged masters of dramatic deceptions, and the shocks which sometimes accompanied their dramas were unforgettable. Kwakiutl theatrical productions were probably unique dramatizations of myths of ancestral origins, and among the devices for such presentations were the three, four, and five face masks (Plates 2, 8A, and 13).

THE KWAKIUTL MASKS

The masks from the various Kwakiutl groups are larger than life. Carvers seemed to dedicate themselves to outdoing one another. The people were extremely competitive in other ways also, especially in the extremes of potlatching. It is significant to point out that although at the time the arts of the tribes were crumbling under the impact of western civilization, the Kwakiutl artist refused to buckle under. Ensconced in remote villages, they continued to carve masks and practice potlatching and other ritual activities dear to them. Chiefs continued to compete in honors and privileges despite the ban imposed on them by the Canadian government.

Kwakiutl masks are full of color and activity, having an exuberance and energy which knows no bounds. Masks are adorned with appendages, projections, and movable parts which reveal remarkable imagin-ation (Plates 16, 25, 33, 53). The face masks are evocative, emotionally laden, often spiritually explosive. Lines are bold elaborations; human features, though recognizable, have marked distortions; yet there are occasional glimpses of mocking or humor that seem to be integral parts of Kwakiutl personality.

Some masks reveal a darker, brooding side; masks with expressions filled with horror; bulging eyes, grimacing mouths, mesmerized stares. Kwakiutl masks had faces placed over movable necks, birds with wing appendages that opened and closed, hiding other faces (Plates 26, 30). Some masks were mechanical wonders; for example, the killer whale mask with double dorsal fins which, though buried in the body of the mask, could spring up when a single string was manipulated (Plate 16). All these appendages were articulated by strings hidden within the mask itself, and pulled by the impersonator.

A powerful element within Kwakiutl masks was that of caricature, the faces that play out the parodies of life. Some masks were meant to terrorize rival chiefs, the so-called ridicule mask (Plate 29). Intra-tribal in nature, it was commissioned by a chief to intimidate a fellow tribesman who dared to challenge him to coveted positions of rank and honor. By making him appear ludicrous to others the chief hoped to demolish the rival's aspirations to his positions.

The Kwakiutl carvers made the largest of all the masks on the North-west Coast. Their secret society masks were of an inter-tribal nature. The Hamatsa (the so-called Cannibal Society) ritual employed masks as large as five feet in length, often weighing almost half as much as the performers who used them. The fantastic masks denoted grades of beings who lived in the house of a fearful spirit. There were complicated Crooked Beaks of the Sky (Plates 12, 13); Hoahoks, or long-beaked ravens (Plate 11), and the Hayth-li-way, forehead masks (Plate 15). Masks were not simply interesting coverings for the face; there was an order in their usage and presentation to the audience, and they were also graded as to rank and symbolism. Profound meanings and functions were associated with each of them.

BELLA COOLA MASKS

The mythologies and folk literature of this group were rich, varied, and in many instances deeply symbolic. Bella Coola masks were masterpieces, but they also represented a distinctive regional style. The carvers were not as inclined towards naturalism as the Tsimshian, nor did they take to the distortions and fantasies characteristic of Kwakiutl art. Bella Coola masks are easy to recognize, as they follow a tradition all their own. Unfortunately, there are not many examples extant in the museums, in contrast to those of other tribes of the Northwest.

Bella Coola masks nearly always had human, or human-like, faces. Masks were of a large size, much larger than those found to the North, and they had heavy, fleshy surfaces. Thick eyebrows and ponderous jowls are characteristic. The enlarged, staring eyes thrust forward from their sockets, bulbous qualities heightened by the rendering of thick full lips (Plate 40). Mouths are ajar, the face arrested as by a sudden surprise. A tension is built into the expressions unlike the refined, often serene, portrait masks of the Tsimshian.

The mask forms of the Bella Coola are powerful representations; the Salmon Bringer mask is a striking example of a transformation type (Plates 9A and 9B). Used in a sacred winter dance called the Kusiut, an inter-tribal religious rite, it survived, by sheer good fortune, the custom followed by the Bella Coola of burning their masks following completion of the ceremonies. They are the only group known to have done this on the Northwest Coast. In burning the sacred masks an incentive was also provided the artists, spurring them to create anew each year the necessary masks for the winter dances. Such a practice also forestalled any tendency toward sterile duplications. Bella Coola masks were not decorated with the exuberant free colors used by the Kwakiutl. The color was more controlled; a light or cobalt blue color often predominated in surface painting.

NOOTKA MASKS

The various tribes residing on the west coast of Vancouver Island constitute the third grouping within the central region. The tribes of the northern area, near the Kwakiutl, seemed to share more affinities with those neighbors than did the groups residing farther to the south. Nootka masks lack the detailed crest and symbolic painting characteristic of those tribes farther to the north. The face masks are naturalistic, but certainly not portrait-like in quality. Facial features lack the detailed surface handling of the north. Effect rather than realism is strong here. Some Nootka tribes employed complicated mechanical masks in secret rituals such as the Klukwalle, the wolf ritual (Plate 19). Many of them are delightful, complicated, almost surrealistic visual expressions, but detailed documentation on function and meaning are lacking for most Nootka masks. However, the spirit of the Bukwis or wild man certainly must have had its stark, tension-laden moments in dance presentations (Plates 23, 24, 35, 36). (Also see below.) Their masks were spare in paint, smaller in size, and of more limited variety than those found among the Kwakiutl or Bella Coola.

CHARACTERISTICS THAT COMMUNICATE

The range of mask types may well be a puzzle for the reader. If there were hundreds of masks used by each tribe, how was it possible for its members to recognize and differentiate one mask from the next? How were masks to be understood and impart their messages to the viewer? How could the people appreciate their meanings?

Types of spirits and characters in history varied from group to group. Each sub-region developed its own beings, culture heroes, ancestors, and benefactors. Neighboring tribes sometimes shared these in common; others developed beings quite unlike those of their neighbors regardless of who they were. The Bella Coola tribes are one such example, for their highly evocative mythologies are anomalous to the other tribes of the Northwest Coast.

Indoctrination of young members of the tribe in the meaning of the symbols of the mythology began at an early age. Young people were expected to become fully conversant with important features of their culture. By the time they were grown they could identify the symbols of their respective lineages within the tribe and differentiate between the crests that were the property of group and those of other kinsmen.

The carvers, knowing no other tradition, worked within the framework of their society's accepted symbolism. The symbols were the clues that provided the viewers with guidelines to their mythic content. They made communication possible. During ceremonial dramas, potlatches, secret society performances—either of an inter-tribal or intra-tribal nature—masks communicated their messages with a strong impact, as anyone who has seen them can testify.

When the artist began merging other-than-human characteristics with the human face he would graft elements onto the human portions in a

Figure A   THUNDERBIRD

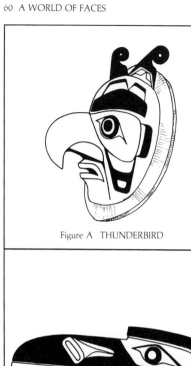

Figure B   RAVEN

Figure C   EAGLE

Figure D   HAWK

Figure E   MOSQUITO

Figure F   KILLER WHALE

number of ways. One way was to put a bird beak where the nose might be; another was to provide the mouth with pointed rather than rounded teeth; still another was to provide the face with two sets of ears, one where human ears are placed, the second pair on the top of the head as one might find on an animal such as wolf or bear. A human face might have a dorsal fin projecting upward from the forehead. While these are simple examples, they are characteristics that helped communicate to the audience the creatures that were intended. But we must remember that human faces did not necessarily represent human beings. They only appeared to do so.

The people believed that in the mythic world of the past, human beings, animals and birds had been able to transform themselves at will. Despite their outward appearances they could communicate between different realms. The masks helped reveal the double nature of their worlds because lurking behind one face was the identity of another creature, perhaps its true character.

A dual interpretation of the masks related to man's association with other living forces in the realms of the past and were a reminder of their common origins. Whales represented not only the great mammal of the sea but, at the same time, the mythological man who created the whales; raven stood for the crest of important clans of the north region and also represented the disguise of the culture hero. Further, raven is given different identities by different tribes: the cannibal raven of the southern Kwakiutl cannot symbolically represent the raven of the Tlingit or Tsimshian. One was a resident in the house of a dreadful, voracious spirit; the other was an agent of the Creator, a hero who moved the world.

To assist the reader, the following examples can be used to clarify symbolism and suggest the significance of the masks. A human face may be portrayed with large horn-like ears located on the top of the face. These forms represent a powerful eagle or thunderbird. (Figure A.) If the beak of the bird is to represent a raven, it will be long and slender, with its tip coming to a point as is illustrated (Figure B). A large beak with sweeping curved thrust which turns down at the end represents the eagle (Figure C), while a smaller beak with a curved downward thrust returning to the mouth or upper lip represents a hawk (Figure D). Bird faces differ from other creatures both in shape and form, but not in size. The mask of a mosquito, prominent in the dramatization of some ancestor origins, has a long and narrow proboscis coming to an abrupt point (Figure E).

There are other creatures popularly depicted in masks, some of which are not quite as easy to recognize. A human face with a dorsal fin appendage projecting from its forehead represents a killer whale (Figure F). Two dorsal fins represent a special supernatural killer whale, a creature from a mythological realm. But dorsal fins may be placed on characters known as sea grizzly bears and sea wolves, no less important than their counterparts on earth. The dual nature of a mask is further revealed by the face which may represent either a person who is affiliated with a member of the killer whale clan of a tribe, or the mythical man who created the killer whales as human beings far in the distant past.

Circular disks on an otherwise clearly human face may represent something totally unrelated to it; this may be the form the giant octopus of the sea takes. Known as Komokwa, he is a popular subject in myths among both the Kwakiutl and Bella Coola peoples (Plates 3, 17, 31). The disks or circular forms represent the sucker cups on its tentacles. The disks also encircle the face or may be confined to a series of round forms stretching across the forehead, as shown in figure G.

There are numerous other forms and images which communicate. Feathers are important clues. A mask with human features, but with feather-like designs on the forehead or below the eyes, represents a raven, eagle, or hawk, depending also on the shape of the beak associated with the face (Figure H). Masks may be with or without ears. Masks may have human faces but with ears placed over the forehead, or with ears in this location and a second set where human beings have them, suggesting bird or animal and human counterparts.

Long narrow projections may extend outward from a face representing the rays of the sun. A sun mask usually has five to seven such projections surrounding the face (Figure I). Yet projections of another type may represent an inhabitant within the realm of the giant octopus, this being the sculpin (Plate 44, top right side; Figure J also).

A human-like face having a vaulted forehead, a turned down mouth, and three or more crescent-shaped forms located in each corner of the mouth or in the middle of the forehead represents a dogfish or shark. (Figure K).

Animals were favorite subjects of mask carvers; the illustrations in this book represent only a few of the types found among the tribes. The northern groups portrayed them generally in benign, friendly repose; the Kwakiutl rendered them more often with fierce and threatening countenances. Animals with long snouts and sharp teeth together with

Figure G GIANT OCTOPUS

Figure J SCULPIN

Figure H EAGLE IN HUMAN FORM

Figure K SHARK OR DOGFISH

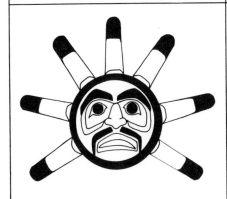

Figure I SUN MASK

Figure L WOLF

Figure M   GRIZZLY BEAR

Figure O   FROG

Figure N   BEAVER

Figure P   TZONOQUA, WILD WOMAN
OF THE FOREST

long, narrow ears are identified as wolves (Figure L). On the other hand, if the mask has a short snout, small ears, sharp or rounded teeth, and, occasionally, a long tongue projecting from between the teeth, a grizzly bear is intended (Figure M). Still smaller snouts with small teeth except for two oversized incisors represent a beaver (Figure N).

A pleasant-appearing creature with round face, no ears, broad lipped mouth and no teeth can be identified as a frog, a very common crest symbol (Figure O). But there are other forms more forbidding. A human-like face with closed eyes or starkly glaring ones, with wild-appearing hair and lips thrust forward, represents the ogress of the forests, the Tzo-no-qua. Her lips are pursed as she gives the lugubrious cry by which she is commonly identified (Figure P). A very human-like mask with pursed lips which are open may be a shaman, however, captured in the act of singing dirges or power songs necessary to communicate with a lost soul.

More frequently found in the northern than the central area are masks representing women. The northern peoples were overwhelmingly matrilineal in descent organization, and women played an unusually important role in the transmission of inheritance, power, status, and prestige. Many northern masks such as the Tsimshian and Haida types (Plates 41 and 45) depict women with large labrets attached to their lower lips, a fashion of the times. Labrets indicated women of unusual rank and importance. The larger the labret the more lofty the woman's role in the tribe; also the more prestigious was her status.

While the examples that have been used do not exhaust the kinds of beings visualized or the symbolism they represent, they do give the reader some awareness of the rich and complicated forms that became a part of the traditional expressions of the Northwest Coast Indians.

THE MEANING OF THE MASKS

It is one thing to be able to identify a mask in terms of the character or spirit intended; it is quite another matter to understand its meaning. Such meanings, which do not cross cultural barriers easily, are the inner content of the mask, embodying deep or spiritual insights which, in turn, rise from the very heart of a people. We can only skim the surface of these but we should try. In so varied a group of masks as are illustrated here, it would be impossible to discuss the complexity of meaning in each. However, in order to convey to the reader the vitality of imagination, the profound perceptions of the seen and unseen world which the masks express, I will focus on a few of them.

THE SALMON BRINGER, Naokx'nim (Plates 9A and 9B).

The mechanical and form characteristics of this mask have been discussed in some detail in Chapter II. As a Bella Coola transformation mask, it is constructed with two separate faces, the outer mask representing the spirit of the salmon. The four appendages symbolize each of four species which spawn in the rivers; there is spring salmon, referred to as "the one that changes itself"; the sockeye, called "the one that penetrates to the head of the river"; the coho, "the one that makes us fat"; and the chinook. The face of the salmon is attached to strings. When these are pulled the mask comes apart in four separate sections (Figures 13, 14, Chapter II), revealing the deity which brings the salmon to the Bella Coola people. He is known as Naokx-nim, the patron of the most sacred of tribal rituals. He is believed to leave his abode among the salmon people in "That Far Away Ocean Place" in early September. He loads his undersea canoe for the great journey. After a long period of travel the people believe he approaches their shores. Naokx'nim then dips his great spirit canoe, first to one side then to the other, allowing all the salmon he has carried with him to escape and start up the rivers which pass the villages. Sacred rituals commemorate this event, the masked dancers repeating the performances four separate times. The journey and the arrival of the salmon are announced by special couriers. It is a time of rejoicing for all.

THE WILD WOMAN OF THE FORESTS, Tzo-no-qua, (Plate 54).

Here is a much loved and respected supernatural being intertribal in nature, every Kwakiutl Indian village knows about her, and every child growing up Kwakiutl learns about her from infancy. She is represented in the crest of many tribes and her form is depicted on cedar columns everywhere—in the village, on the beaches, in the graveyards, in the potlatch houses. Tzo-no-qua has a two-sided nature; at times fearful and awesome, at other times ridiculous and even stupid. She has a lugubrious cry, Huuuuu, Huuuuu, Huuuuu, which echoes through the stillness of the forests. As a benefactress she has been known to bestow supernatural gifts and wealth on those fortunate enough to have chanced to meet her.

But she is also the source of terror for small children for she is known as the nightmare bringer.

There are numerous subtle variations of this face, each serving a particular ritual or ceremonial function. The face depicted (Plate 32) is a smaller version and is known as a gi-kumlth. It is used for one purpose and one purpose alone, to formally bring to a close a potlatch proceeding. The first time I saw one in use I was stunned.

The gi-kumlth Tzo-no-qua mask is restricted to a very special use by the chiefs who are hosting potlatches. Before all the guests and rivals, the host stands. He bends his knees in a low crouch, the mask held over his face. He gives the cry of the Tzo-no-qua. Everyone gets up and starts for home. But this being also represents awesome supernatural power. She is not just another forest spirit who abducts children and eats them. Eating is symbolic of wealth and this act symbolized her incredible powers; her appetite, her feeding, her feasting, the feasting of the people. She is deeply imprinted in the Kwakiutl mind, oriented as it is to food, the giving of gifts, and the distribution of wealth. It is appropriate that she signals the end of the potlatch in which so much had been eaten and given away.

THE RULER OF THE UNDERSEA, Komokwa, (Plates 3, 17, 21 and 28).

Though this mask is used inter-tribally, the rites associated with it might be of an intra-tribal nature. The Northwest Coast Indians had visions of many types of beings who were associated with the ocean and often lived in it. Among them none was as powerful or more feared than Komokwa, the giant octopus. Kwakiutl say he lives in a great house made of copper under the sea. Its roof is held up by columns of sea lions, his attendants. His pets are the seals. Komokwa controlled the coming and going of all who lived within his watery realm. He was also known as the destroyer of men who ventured on the seas without proper propitiations. Komokwa's children became the ancestors of some of the Kwakiutl lineages. Appendages adorn his mask forms, with symbolic tentacles; sucker cups, movable figures which rotate such as loon, sawbill ducks, sea gulls, and sculpins. Komokwa played an important part in the winter dances and many families took his mask as a crest. During potlatches he entered the great house from the beach. With cries of surprise the chiefs present would rise and sing his songs. "Oh welcome, honorable chief of the sea." The orator told the audience that the undersea king has visited the chief who was descended from his illustrious ancestors. A dramatic performance follows which captures the spirit of this revelation. Finally, Komokwa retires behind a screen partition, leaving the audience marveling.

THE EAGLE OF THE UNDERSEA, Kwikwis, (Plate 1).

This magnificent creature resides in the ocean and is claimed by several Kwakiutl families as a valued family crest. It is an intra-tribal mask but during inter-tribal potlatches was exhibited in dances. These masks are also very large, sometimes weighing over fifty pounds complete with its entire costume. The outer face of this transformation mask represents the eagle, Kwikwis. When strings are pulled it breaks into three separate parts, revealing an inner face which is identified as the sun hawk. The opening of the outer face activates a series of appendages symbolizing the sun's rays which surround the inner face; indeed, a transformation from eagle to sun.

Well-calculated effects precede the entrance of Kwikwis at a potlatch. The beat of sticks on the cedar log drums grows faster, louder. There is an air of expectation. Screams split the air, interrupting the potlatch proceedings. Men rush into the house to announce that a great and terrible bird has risen from the ocean depths and is this minute walking on the beach as if awaiting an appointed hour. The host turns to his audience to announce that his great lineage's crest has finally come. He sends his attendants to bid the bird to enter his house. Stalking as an eagle does, one foot slowly in front of the other, the impressive creature comes closer to the fire. The eyes of the audience are riveted on his every feature from giant talons to great copper teeth. Then the Kwikwis turns counterclockwise, moving towards the row of chieftains who are the guests. It whirls, pulling the eagle mask strings, revealing the inner face, a transformation as if by magic. The chorus of singers then begin the song associated with the undersea eagle. The ritual is enacted four times so that everyone in the great house can witness the transformation. The moving parts must operate with split-second unity; the snapping shut and opening of the outside face must be done with precision. The audience responds as though witnessing a miraculous event. The Kwikwis then retires behind the screen while an orator explains the story of the acquisition of this crest by the host's ancestors. The performer for such a dance must be carefully chosen. No mere youth will do. He must be a mature adult of large frame, strong, and in top condition for only such a person can carry the weight of the mask and the costume and do the body-turning, leaping, and high-stepping dance necessary for such a performance.

THE RIDICULE MASK, (Plate 28).

During the height of rivalries in potlatching in the 1870s and 1880s, masks of this type were not uncommon. They were worn by kinsmen of a chief who was potlatching, its nature being an inter-tribal affair. The mask was carved for the host in a blatant attempt to intimidate and ridicule a rival chief who challenged him for a coveted position.

The confrontations occurred when the host feasted his enemy while at the same time exposing him to ridicule. This particular mask represents an unfortunate chief whose face is slowly melting away from the heat of his host's fire. Kwakiutl chiefs often followed the practice of pouring ladles of expensive eulachon oil over the flames, a gesture of disdain for their own wealth. As the oil fueled the flames, generating great heat, the rival who had purposely been seated close to the fire suffered terribly yet dared not move away. He would lose face and bring dishonor to his lineage if he were to acknowledge publicly the superior wealth of his host.

By pouring oil over the fire and "melting the rival" a host showed his power, his wealth, in effect melting away *all* rivals who dared to challenge him.

Every mask in this volume, every mask extant,—and these number in the several thousands—has a story to tell. Many of them, the ridicule mask being an example, require an in-depth knowledge of the customs and values of the people, in order to understand their deeper meanings. Others can be appreciated and understood with a general knowledge of the character of the cultural milieu of the Northwest Coast tribes.

THE HOST AND HIS MASKS

Tribes continually competed to outdo one another in depicting their myths or displaying their prized possessions. Whether for secret society uses or for inter- or intra-tribal potlatches, or for both, masks were sources of intense specialization and pride. They were shown to audiences at great cost, also with great risks involved. The host had to convey to the artist the nature of his people's possessions, the pride and symbolism involved, and the artist was required to capture their essence. Neither artist nor host could fail.

When presented in its proper context a mask must bring the owner esteem, enhance the pride of his family and lineage, and be a source of envy from others, not of his own group alone. It must sway an audience so that the people are astounded by what they see. The impersonator also played a vital role in bringing the drama to its finest moments. The spirits must be believable in their movements, gestures, and in the timing of the dance steps to the drum beats and the rhythm of the chorus. Masks achieve the impossible, becoming (to their audience) not only plausible but downright believable. The impersonator lets the spirit of the mask take over. Through his actions and his power the spirit commands the audience to respond favorably through the elements of suspense, timing, surprise, striking expression, visual novelty, and the power of symbolism. A host watched the reactions of his guests very closely, particularly the rival leaders who were present. Will the masks work? Will the power of his crests and the symbols of his tribe overwhelm the people?

If the masks achieve an hypnotic sway over the audience, the intensity of the drama reaches a crescendo. The opening masks, the surprise, the stirring quality of their meanings, should send a ripple—no, a unified gasp—through the audience. That is the moment of truth. It is the time the host chief has been waiting for. He smiles. His people are proud.

If the timing is not synchronized correctly, if the faces do not break open evenly or close with a sharp crack, or if the strings become entangled or worse, break, it is a sad day for the host and his family. They will be the butts of ridicule and derision.

On the other hand, if these expectations are realized the swelling of pride knows no bounds. One chief, a Kwakiutl, watched his potlatch come to an end. He observed the audience still in obvious shock from the presentation of his masks and crests. He went over to the carver who had been sitting unobtrusively in the audience and was overheard to say to him:

> "You have brought me such honor! Your masks have brought my
> name such honor! Let me pay you again for the work you have
> done for me. Here, take this fistful of money. Take more!"

As the host he was doing the honorable thing. Paying the artist double his original fee brought him greater prestige because the desired ends had been achieved with such stunning impact.

THE AUDIENCE

The audience witnessing such proceedings was made up of both the aristocratic families and the commoners, people of low rank and status, together with others whom I call the uninitiated, i.e. children, ordinary women, the lower classes in general. They didn't fully comprehend what these performances were all about. But all the audience understood that the more important the host's crests and wealth, the greater were his risks, the finer the moment for the artist, the higher the prestige for both himself and his patron.

It was important that all the people should witness the novelty of the mask, the wonder it conveyed, and the envy it aroused in those power-hungry rival leaders who hated to be outshone. Humbled rivals from different tribes often left such proceedings with vows to outdo their host no matter what it took in the way of expenditures. These inter-tribal and intra-tribal activities fueled the fires of competition and artistic excellence. The audience watched the masked performances for evidence of perfection of the impersonators' movements, gestures, the believability of the spirit portrayed, the lack of mechanical failures, the crisp opening and closing of the masks. There must be no falls, no stumbling, no hesitation of movement. The features of a mask must be recognizable, the whale an authentic whale, the ghost a proper ghost, the eagle a convincing eagle. If the artistry of the masks was of a high order, then for a few brief minutes, the audience had a vision of the world they were certain existed; for had not the evidence for such existence been affirmed year after year, generation after generation, leading back to the spirit ancestors?

THE UNINITIATED VIEW THE MASKS

Usually women and children had no access of any kind to the esoteric knowledge associated with the masks. Theoretically, they must never be exposed to the truth of the sources or the impersonations. The higher-ranking women knew of the mask uses, of course, as some were their inherited property. For the women of lower rank and commoners, the masks were supposed to be real creatures that resided elsewhere but who visited the people at appointed hours. The impact of such creatures on the children can be imagined. But cradled in their parents' arms and reassured, they come to view the masked figures as part of the real world around them. From the earliest age, they heard the names, listened to the stories, acquired respect for the masks and, under the proper circumstances, even learned which ones to avoid. In not a few of these dramas, however, the wail of a child pierced the air while total attention of the audience centered upon the performers. That was something to experience.

HOW I SAW THE AUDIENCE

I have had the good fortune to watch several winter dances and potlatches performed among the Kwakiutl of Vancouver Island. Hosts and guests were friendly and hospitable. The openhanded generosity so characteristic of the people continues to prevail. Even a stranger within their midst is given gifts by the host during the distribution of wealth to guests.

When masked performers enter the great halls, a hush falls over the audience as they watch all the details of the dance and costumes. The appearance of the masks come as a surprise since the program is not announced beforehand. As acknowledged masters of a stagecraft Kwakiutl hosts have not lost their age-old sense of theater, which even includes skill with visual puns. While the dances and masked dramas have somber content, I have witnessed superb techniques for relieving the tensions that build up during the performance. Serious sequences alternate with light-hearted antics, even downright burlesque-like turns which send the audience into fits of laughter. Potlatches are not the places to find withdrawn or moody Indians. Far from it; they consider themselves equal to all, superior to most, and they show it. The audience has often traveled a long way to be entertained, to be moved by what they see, and to enjoy deep belly laughs. These are the good parts of living and the people know the good life when they experience it.

During the height of some rituals, members of the audience—either male or female, depending on the dance—jump into the dancing area. They have become mesmerized by the power of the dancers' gestures or the rhythmic staccato beat, or even the words of the songs that are being sung. They jump from their seats and dance along the sidelines, performing their own distinctive interpretations of the spirit. I once saw several men performing the dance of the novice during the Cannibal Society initiation. They had all done it before perhaps several times, and it brought back to them deeply personal and satisfying experiences.

CHAPTER V

DEATH AND REBIRTH OF THE MASK

I t is an irony that mask making and the accompanying dramatic arts throve and flourished so richly just as Indian societies were entering a critical period which threatened their very existence. The nineteenth century was a time of continuous and rapid change as the region came under the hegemony of whites representing powerful new political, economic and technological forces which challenged the Indian for supremacy in his own land. By the middle of the century these radical changes had already begun to sweep aside the very foundations of Northwest Indian life though the outward manifestations had not yet fully appeared. The nature of these changes were vast and complex, and of such magnitude that the people were totally unprepared to understand or even cope with them. (For example, the 1884 Canadian legislation forbidding potlatching.) The tribes faced cultural and racial extinction.

Rene D'Harnoncourt, late director of the Museum of Modern Art in New York, once summarized the nature of contacts between the Indian worlds of America and the white man's civilization when he wrote:

> "The Anglo-Saxon smashes the native culture wherever he comes into contact with it, and then with infinite patience and care gathers up the pieces and enshrines them behind glass."

Many questions remain to be answered. Why did the art of mask making collapse? Did all the tribes succumb at the same time? What happened to the carvers and their patrons? What about the institutions which nourished the carvers, the societies, potlatches, shamanistic rituals?

For several decades the trade goods that the whites brought in return for native furs, labor, and fish, enhanced the Indians' material well-being and stimulated the growth of certain social institutions as well as their arts. An artificial euphoria brought the people a sense of prosperity as goods added wealth to their lineages; potlatches grew more frequent in numbers, carvers prospered with commissions, leaders reached for the heights. Wealth exchanged hands numerous times. But there were unanticipated effects which became disastrous. The easy access to coveted goods stimulated a spiraling rivalry between factions within tribes and between tribes themselves. It intensified centuries-old animosities and suspicions. The access to guns and gunpowder increased inter-tribal raiding and warfare. As if these factors were not liabilities enough, numerous diseases were introduced by maritime traders and settlers. The tribes had little previous exposure to them and had developed no immunity.

Within the decades from 1860 to 1900 the Northwest Coast tribes were ravaged; whole regions became depopulated, villages by the scores totally abandoned. Thousands died of smallpox, measles, tuberculosis, even malaria. Such a drastic reduction in population occurred that several large tribal groups were threatened with extinction. Once dominant powers such as the Chinook of the lower Columbia River, the Haida of the Queen Charlotte Islands, and the Bella Coola along the central coast literally disappeared before the end of the nineteenth century.

White man's goods of every imaginable type and fancy inundated the Indians' world. Gradually these, together with other pressures, began to undermine the values of the people in countless ways. They helped break down lines of authority established within lineages. They snapped the rules that governed protocol within the tribe; crumbled and eroded sanctions led to the weakening of links of responsibility; unity and loyalty to lineage and clan began to loosen. Pretenders to high rank jockeyed for power, or challenged those who were traditionally entrusted with inherited rights. Nightmares of uncontrolled change were followed by dissolution through alcohol and widespread confusion. Once proud institutions and traditional practices with deep meanings for the tribes were undermined, even ridiculed. Leaders were discredited, their authority and moral mandates evaporated.

Newly imposed systems of law introduced by American and Canadian authorities supplanted the old; new values about private and public property replaced the old; new rules for redress of wrongs, inherited rights, individual initiative, an economy based on working hard, hoarding—these and a hundred more foreign customs left the people stymied, frustrated, and bewildered. One of the most destructive blows was the missionary effort to stamp out the people's religious and spiritual beliefs. The grand design was to convert the heathens to Christianity and replace the traditional customs and practices with those used by the dominant culture. Before conversion was possible, however, it was necessary to root out all vestiges of the past which the Indians seemed reluctant to give up.

Naturally, the first institution threatened was the potlatch. It seemed to symbolize all aboriginal evils rolled into one: its disposal of wealth, its masked performances, its dances, patrons, artists, ancestors, spirits, deities, demons, ghosts, etc. The arts of all kinds were vital targets to be crushed because they were the visual means of transmitting the ancient spiritual traditions. From totem poles to community houses, from feast dishes to dancing regalia, from songs and poetry to tribal languages—all were marked for destruction. The zeal directed towards the extirpation of these practices was matched only by the geographic extent of their effort.

I am reminded of the experience narrated by the writer, Katharine Kuh, in an article in the *Saturday Review;* "The First Americans As Artists." She had gone to the deserted Haida village of Kasaan in search of totem poles which might yet be standing *in situ* in the mid 1950 s. An elderly missionary woman approached her cautiously. "Be you a teacher?" "No," she answered. "Be you a missionary?" "No." "Be you a prostitute?" "No." "Well, what brought you here?" she asked. Kuh's answer stunned her. She had come to study totem pole art. For this woman the Indians were incapable of providing art. They were heathen children whose ungodly carvings were better burned and forgotten. Her whole effort, Kuh points out, was directed toward utterly destroying the very objects Kuh had traveled so far to see.

I had a similar experience in a Kwakiutl village in 1946. A pastor had asked me why I had come to this village. My answer was "to study Indian art." He said there were no arts worth studying here. Little did he know.

Government administrators, religious leaders, and settlers alike felt that rooting out the culture of the Indian would render a service, preparing them for the road to enlightenment and civilization. Little effort was made to understand the underpinnings of the potlatch, for example, which touched on generosity and sharing, as well as competition, or the myriad intangibles that provided the Indians with joy, beauty, or security. Pressure was relentless—both covertly and overtly applied.

Gradually an enormous body of social customs passed from the scene as tribe after tribe converted to Christianity. The patrons had no further need for the artists to carve the masks and other ceremonial paraphernalia; the artists lost their patrons and, therefore, the reasons for their skills. Even the shaman was discredited; he could not cure people any more. He had lost his powers. New circumstances made old customs obsolete in the entire southern British Columbia and northern Washington state northward to the Haida, Tlingit, and Tsimshian country. With the passing of the potlatches and membership in secret societies, the songs, dances, masks, stagecraft techniques were no longer necessary.

The degree and speed of conversion varied with many factors, the remoteness of the settlement, the intensity of external pressures, the depth of resistance to change, or commitment to tribal institutions. In the north, Haida almost vanished in British Columbia as small remnants hovered about two settlements in the Queen Charlottes. The Tsimshian and Tlingit tribes, with but one or two exceptions, converted to Christian beliefs, purging themselves at least outwardly of aboriginal ties. The arts of mask carving so deeply entrenched in the past fell into disuse. The Bella Coola did not survive the contact with the white man, and have almost disappeared as a tribe.

The southern Kwakiutl and Nootkans survived in some remote areas, refusing to accept all but the outward trappings of western culture. The Kwakiutl remained defiant. Many groups continued potlatching, participating in secret society rites, mask carving, and dancing arts. Disapproval, punishments, even legal sanctions failed to convince them that their customs were wrong. The Canadian Indian Act of 1884 forbidding potlatching did not stop them. But what missionaries and administrators could not do, economic laws almost succeeded in doing. The lowest point was reached both culturally and in population during the World Depression of the 1930s.

Another dimension must be considered as a factor in the decline of mask making. As tribal populations fell and missionary zeal increased, Indian cultures headed for collapse, as we have seen. Anthropologists were aware of this fact and became concerned about gathering the last vestiges of these Northwest Indian cultures for historical documentation. Scientists and field collectors began converging on the Northwest Coast from both Europe and America about the turn of the century, gathering together enormous collections of artifacts, the bulk of which were masks and ceremonial equipment. Many Indians were only too glad to oblige collectors by getting rid of their lineage masks and other heirlooms which were useless in the new social and religious order. Besides they made a profit. The physical remnants of these cultures were then assembled in large collections for future research and analysis, but in the process entire settlements were depleted of masks. In the meantime numerous carvers had died with no apprentices trained to replace them, so this massive collecting, while preserving artifacts, accelerated the decline of the arts. Collectors like Bastien of Germany, Boas from Columbia University, the Emmonses (father and son), Niblack, Barrett, Rasmussen, and a hundred others assembled huge collections, thousands of masks in fact, which eventually found homes in major institutions throughout the world.

With the population decline tribes could not fill the positions which would have kept the various institutions functioning in a traditional manner. Nor could they gather the wealth necessary to validate claims to unoccupied positions. Custom after custom associated with masked performances and prerogatives withered away and disappeared.

It is interesting to examine the Indians' responses to collectors. Like the responses to missionaries and to the pressures for conversion, these varied from group to group and tribe to tribe. Many Tlingits and Tsimshian tribes renounced their possessions of the past and embraced the new ways, while other groups refused to part with a single object, a single mask, regardless of promises or price. The Kwakiutl responded in another way, providing us with additional insight into their tenacity, ingenuity, and adaptability. They often sold their ritual masks to visiting collectors, charging what for those days seemed exorbitant prices. They then turned about, pocketed some of the profit in order to enhance their future potlatching prospects, and then commissioned carvers to make more masks. But for the Tlingit the original mask was the treasure and heirloom; no copies could be tolerated. For the Kwakiutl, it was the symbol or the idea of the crest that was owned, and so that was what counted. The object could be duplicated again and again, the more unusual and different the better. Kwakiutl mask carving endured; it did not die out; it continued to be practiced *sub-rosa* as innovators within the tribes searched for new ways to express their skills. The practice all but disappeared among the other tribes. At the turn of the twentieth century the Kwakiutl entered a new phase of productivity and innovativeness which matched and even surpassed earlier expressions. So productive were they that one major university museum filled its entire collection with examples made for the most part within this time period.

BELATED RECOGNITION OF THE MASKS AS ART

Ethnographers and artists were first drawn to the arts of Northwest Coast mask making, having become aware of their inherent vitality long before the general public became acquainted with them. But their interests and appreciation stemmed from different perceptions. The ethnographers were scientifically oriented; for them masks posed problems with respect to motivations, functions, and meanings within preliterate tribal societies. The artists looked at the masks as aesthetic expressions, as creative forms with a powerful visual impact. They noted a superb grasp of line, texture, design and color. They were only mildly interested in what they represented or what their deeper meanings signified.

The natural history museums established collections for scientific inquiry and historical documentation, but few art museums recognized any aesthetic values in these arts until about 1950. But Northwest Coast masks were exposed to the general public in increasing numbers starting in earnest with the San Francisco World's Fair of 1934. Yet even by the 1940s Northwest art was not widely collected.

By the 1950s greater interest resulted from a number of major exhibitions of this art around the United States, e.g. at the Denver Art Museum, and the Colorado Springs Fine Arts Center, and the Seattle World's Fair in 1962. The Portland Art Museum had acquired the Rasmussen collection in 1948. The Denver Art Museum began collecting in earnest in the late 1940s and early '50s. These were the pace-setters. Recognition of fine public collections in British Columbia was belated but in recent years, the Provincial Museum, the University Museum, and the Vancouver Centennial Museum have developed stunning displays. Exhibitions of national scope were held in quick succession during the 1960s at the Art Institute of Chicago, the Lowie Museum in Berkeley, California, the Whitney Museum in New York, the Vancouver Art Gallery and the National Gallery of Art in Washington, D.C., to name just a few. Masks played a major part in all these exhibits; connoisseurs and art museum directors began to take notice. As more interest was shown, prices of masks rose, eventually rocketing out of sight. The cycle was completed when men of wealth, now representing Western culture rather than tribal cultures, began competing for ownership of coveted examples, or strove to be benefactors of museums with bestowal of gifts. Art museums began contending for ownership of outstanding examples of this art; an avalanche of books followed; photographic essays, pamphlets, leaflets, all began inundating publishers' lists. Most dealt rather superficially with the masks and the other arts of the Northwest Coast tribes, nor was there enough serious exploration of the dynamics which stimulated the development of this unique art form.

NEW ARTISTS, NEW TRENDS

Mask collecting by research institutions depleted the possessions of most villages, but for some tribes collecting encouraged carvers to continue their output. The southern Kwakiutl was one such group. While only four men are singled out as examples, it is certain that many more continued to work, providing stunning masks for patrons. The four were Charlie James, Willie Sewid, Mungo Martin, and George Wa'kus.

Charles James (Yakuglas was his Indian name) was a major innovator, the son of a Fort Rupert Kwakiutl woman and a white American sawmill owner from Port Townsend. When James' mother died he was only seven years old. His mother's tribe adopted him, rearing him as an Indian. Through her line he inherited rights to carve and was trained by a kinsman. As a mature man in the early 1920s James began to teach carving to the youngest members of his family. He introduced new concepts, new forms, new color use, all of which took hold among receptive kinsmen. His influence was immense and it continued with his stepson Mungo Martin. James' stepdaughter Ellen Newman Neal (Ka ka solas) also learned carving from him. She found her greatest productivity in the decade prior to her death in 1966.

When I observed Mungo Martin (Nakap'unkim) between 1945 and 1950 in Fort Rupert he was carving masks for patrons who lived in neighboring villages such as Kingcome Inlet, Alert Bay, and Village Island. In turn, as he prepared to potlatch, he commissioned other carvers to make his crest masks. It was inappropriate for a carver who potlatched to make his own.

Mungo exerted great influence on other Kwakiutl, as he was not only a chieftain but a man of respected status, wisdom, and leadership. He stood rooted in his traditional heritage but he was adaptive to change.

The Canadian government hired him as a senior carver in the mid- 1950s in the totem pole restoration project at the Provincial Museum. Other carvers, like Henry Hunt, Tony Hunt, Douglas Cranmer and Bill Reid, learned from him. I feel that I do an injustice here to other carvers he influenced whose names I failed to record.

Projects similar to those initiated in Canada began among the Tlingit in Alaska. The U.S. Interior Department encouraged Tlingit carvers with research materials, equipment, working space, and consulting services. The Tsimshian carvers under the aegis of a local settler started a training program in mask carving at the historic site of Ksan on the Skeena River. This project was greatly encouraged by Mrs. Polly Sargent of Hazelton, B.C. The recent skills revealed by this group are startling and suggest that mask making among them is in a healthy state of revival.

Another carver of profound influence was Willie Sewid (Haytla'mis) of Blunden Harbor. His colleague in mask carving was George Wa'kus from the same village. Wa'kus unfortunately remains an enigma as little research has focused on him, but he was a master of single faces as well as Crooked Beaks, such as his example illustrated in Plate 13.

Sewid, on the other hand, was a master carver of secret society masks. His influence spread among tribes of the Kwakiutl from 1900 to 1950. Sewid's genius centered around the large ritual masks of ravens, Cannibal Ravens, and Crooked Beaks (Plates 11, 12, 14). He introduced new forms, ornate elaborations, and a proliferation of surface designs which found favor among a growing number of patrons.

By 1951 a new Indian Act has been passed by the Canadian government which pointedly omitted any mention of the potlatch. A resurgence of activity followed which had a ripple effect up and down the coast. A renewal of potlatching and other social ceremonies started with the use of crest symbols and masks, calling for new expenditure of energies in order to renew the tradition of art forms. Another generation of carvers stepped forward, led by a working group of older men familiar with the traditional techniques, tools, and perceptions of the past. The continuity between past and present, though seriously impaired, had not been completely broken after all. Partly due to the work of remarkably gifted white men who understood the design forms of the Northwest Coast style, carving had undergone a tremendous upsurge. Bill Holm, Curator of Northwest Coast Indian Art, Burke Memorial Museum at the University of Washington, and Duane Pasco of Seattle should be singled out for their contributions to this resurgence. The late Wilson Duff, Professor of Anthropology at the University of British Columbia, did much to stimulate Indian recognition of their heritage.

In the 1960s government policies both in Canada and the United States took a drastic about-face. Recognition of the rights of Indian and Eskimo minorities as citizens gained momentum, and government goals now sought to enlighten the public as well as encourage Indian minorities in their respect for the past and pride in their identity and heritage (Indians now wish to be known as Native Americans). Encouragement to pursue their arts followed. In the field of education new interest in Native American and Eskimo cultures took root; bilingual teaching of minority children in the lower grades became a part of education policy; individual respect for the children's cultural past was encouraged. Employment opportunities were stepped up. More pride and appreciation in Indian history, oral literature, dance, and languages was revived among these people who had all but forgotten them. From the latter nineteenth century to the latter twentieth century, the attitudes of the dominant society have been completely reversed.

A NEW CULTURAL HERITAGE

Destruction of cultures does not abate around the globe, but in our century it is accompanied by widespread indignation and a corresponding cherishing of peoples whose identity is imperilled. Intelligent interest in alien cultures and the compassion that goes with it is more marked now than at any time in the past. We are ourselves less certain of what constitutes a good life and no longer so confident that our own restless, highly technological life patterns are necessarily best.

But much damage has been done. White men, mostly Americans and Canadians, have tampered radically with the lives of the Northwest Coast Indians, leaving a trail of resentment and bitterness among them. And with reason, for we know—and they do—that the energy and vitality once inherent in their culture has been deeply compromised, its remarkable creative exuberance muffled, its will-to-be critically weakened.

Have we in fact witnessed its death? Is there such a thing as the resurrection of a culture? Can the Northwest tribal societies somehow turn back the clock, recreating the vibrant culture their great grandparents knew? We know they cannot. The work of missionaries, the doctrine of manifest destiny, inescapable technological advances, simple greed, and finally government bureaucrats, have had their irreversible effect.

Yet, in spite of all this, there is growing evidence that more has remained alive in some of the tribes than we would have imagined possible after this onslaught. More tribes than the Kwakiutl have found ways to circumvent the white man's authority, his laws, and his overwhelming presence. If tribal cultures are utterly moribund why is there a significant resurgence in mask making and in the traditional use of masks again, in potlatches and ritual dances? These events are not for the white man's benefit; they are for the Indians themselves. And why the assumption of names, prerogatives, crests, and lineage ties again? These too seem not to have died out after all. Many of the languages spoken remain intact; in fact, the younger generation appears to be learning to speak them as eagerly as their parents rejected them a generation or two ago.

Potlatches have been revived and have begun to appear with increasing frequency. Between 1960 and 1975, for example, scores of potlatches were given among the Kwakiutl, one following the other during winter months. I can count over twenty-eight that I personally know about, including the names of the hosts and an idea of the approximate amounts given away; a few exceeded several thousands of dollars. I witnessed several, and I made mental notes of the procedures and protocol followed, all of which conjured up images of Franz Boas' classic descriptions published in 1895. Obviously they have not been irretrievably lost, after all.

Seating arrangements, for example, followed traditional patterns with commoners near the front doors of the great houses, chiefs and other dignitaries near the rear screen; ceremonies conducted in Kwakwalla, the language of the people; speeches and speech forms of impressive eloquence, gesture, imagery, punctuated with high praise and traditional double meanings; the use of eulachon oil poured over fires to show disdain for wealth; the use of "talking sticks" when guests narrated the greatness of the host's family; the use of traditional dance steps, songs, choruses, together with their paraphernalia; the piling up of gifts in large mounds prior to distributing so that they would make an impressive sight; the honoring of the names of the dead; the surprise and feigned terror, produced by stagecraft techniques well designed to both entertain and awe an audience. The flowery speeches, the tension building in the audience as the masked dancers perform, the exhibiting of crests; and the emphasis place on food and wealth are all still present. The connections with the old culture, however weakened, have clearly not been severed. Remembered rituals, remaining artifacts, and the handskills of a gifted race, are still there.

The changed views of the last decade made many of us more sensitive toward all minorities, but especially toward Indians, and a new assertiveness on the part of the Native Americans themselves has also modified public attitudes. The massive indifference of the past is dissolving. A much wider public now knows and appreciates the powerful and fully evolved art of the Northwest Indians—especially the superb masks. This more perceptive public can look forward to new experiences with the art of the present day carvers whose masks are the more precious to us because their tradition, so near extinction, somehow survived. It seems to come naturally to the hands of carvers whose ancestors evolved an art easily comparable to the greatest art in wood produced by any other culture in any period.

Plate 1 FAMILY CREST MASK

Kwakiutl, northern Vancouver Island, B.C., late 19th cent. *Transformation mask:* this is a superb example of the lengths patron and artist will reach in order to capture the awe-inspiring theatrical qualities of a supernatural benefactor. The great mask represents Kwikwis, the eagle of the undersea. The outer face breaks into several parts at the beak. The inner face has an explosive effect upon the viewer and is identified as a hawk, symbolizing the sun. Both eagle and hawk crests were treasured family possessions, being closely tied with experiences ancestors had with mythic beings.

Courtesy Milwaukee Public Museum, Wisconsin.

Plate 2 FAMILY CREST MASK

Kwakiutl, northern Vancouver Island, B.C., late 19th cent. *Transformation mask:* the face is in two parts, the large structure above it is compressed and is not initially seen. Hidden strings articulate the outer face, breaking it into two separate parts while strings pull the painted muslin backing so that it opens like a sail catching a full wind. The small carved figure moves its arms in the manner of a puppet. The mask represents the sun, with the inside face symbolizing the sun's inner spirit.

Courtesy Museum of the American Indian, New York.

Plate 3 FAMILY CREST MASK

Kwakiutl, northern Vancouver Island, B.C., early 20th cent. *Mechanical type:* the numerous disks bordering the head represent the sucker cups on the tentacles of the giant octopus, Komokwa. The shield-like forms hanging from the chin represent coppers, symbols of great wealth. The small figures on the head represent dwellers in Komokwa's realm. They gyrate when hidden strings are pulled.

Courtesy Vancouver Centennial Museum, Vancouver, B.C.

Plate 4 FAMILY CREST MASK

Nootka, western Vancouver Island, B.C., late 19th-early 20th cent. *Mechanical type:* represents the sun. The face and round flat disk above it are carved from alder. When the disk breaks into two parts, ten triangular cedar rays spread out and encircle the head. Eyes open and close.

Courtesy Vancouver Centennial Museum, Vancouver, B.C.

Plate 5   MASKED PERFORMERS OF THE KWAKIUTL

This Curtis photograph, destined to be one of his most famous, shows us how performers looked in general but it does not show a specific performance. Most masks are family crest types. Included are a sea eagle, mountain goat, wild man, grizzly bear, killer whale, wasp, bee, and raven. In the center foreground are several types of bird masks used in the cannibal society dance. In the background on left and right are carved crest poles while in the rear center is a distinctive column called hamspek. The performer enters the house through the roof, wiggling down through the holes in the pole until he reaches the floor. The presentation of numerous masks such as these takes considerable time, as each has its own characteristics, songs, steps, and action.

Photograph by Edward Curtis, North American Indians, Volume X, 1915.

Plate 6 A GROUP OF MASKED KWAKIUTL
DANCERS

Crest masks are usually presented to an audience
singly rather than as here in a posed photograph
showing a mixture of masks. The masks represented
include a sculpin (fish), sea eagle, Tzo-no-qua spirit (behind the flukes of the killer whale in the center of
photograph), a mountain goat, two grizzly bears, two
killer whales. While it is a staged photograph it does
capture an overall atmosphere of the masked performers.

*Photograph by Edward Curtis, North American In-
dians, Volume X, 1915.*

Plate 7 MASKED DANCERS FROM SOUTH-
ERN KWAKIUTL TRIBES

Two squatting dancers wearing masks associated with
the cannibal secret society dance. The performer on
the right wears the long-beaked Cannibal Raven mask;
the one on the left another bird prominent in the performance. The strips of red cedar bark of both coarse
and finely shredded strands cover the dancers' bodies.
Beaks of the masks open and close with sharp clacking
sounds by strings held in the dancers' hands (Figure
18).

*Photograph by Edward Curtis, North American In-
dians, Volume X, 1915.*

Plates 8A & 8B FAMILY CREST MASK

Kwakiutl, northern Vancouver Island, B.C., late 19th cent. *Transformation mask:* outer mask represents the bullhead frog; in the center a raven appears. The inner mask represents an ancestor. Each face in turn breaks into two equal parts cleverly revealing another creature. Each mask is hinged and the manipulation of hidden strings allows the impersonator to control the opening or closing of each face. In ceremonies such masks present stunning dramatic effects.

Courtesy American Museum of Natural History, New York.

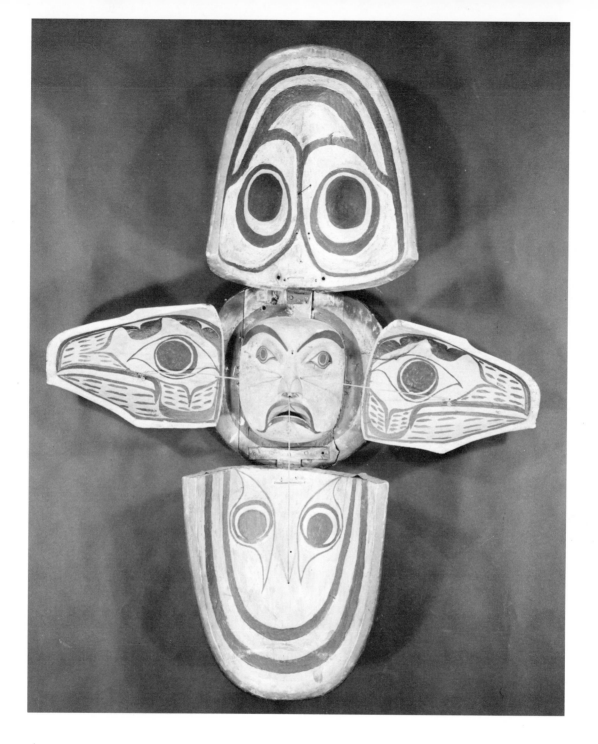

Plates 9A & 9B   SECRET SOCIETY MASK

Bella Coola: central British Columbia, late 19th cent.
Transformation mask: one of a series of masks used
in the Kusiut Society, which held sacred autumn
thanksgiving rites. The outer face represents the
salmon. It has four appendages in salmon form which
open and close. When opened (B) the inner face represents the reverent bringer of the salmon known as
Noakx'nim.

*Courtesy American Museum of Natural History,
New York.*

Plate 10 FAMILY CREST MASK

Kwakiutl, northern Vancouver Island, B.C., late 19th-early 20th cent. *Transformation mask:* used in the winter ceremonies called Lao Laxa. The outer face breaks into three separate parts revealing a second face with prominent beak. It symbolizes the hawk associated with the sun. The outer mask represents the sun behind clouds, the inner mask (the hawk face) is the sun in clear sky. The four projections represent sun rays but have an additional function of providing necessary leverage to open and close the outer face.

*Courtesy Vancouver Centennial Museum,
Vancouver, B.C.*

Plate 11 SECRET SOCIETY MASK

Kwakiutl, northern Vancouver Island, B.C., late 19th cent. *Mechanical type:* more than five feet in length, this mask represents the cannibal raven. This is one of several types used in the winter dance. Masks of such length require the performer to be harnessed into the mask to avoid accidents. Some assistance is also necessary to guide him about the performing area.

Courtesy Portland Art Museum, Oregon.

Plate 12 SECRET SOCIETY MASK

Kwakiutl, northern Vancouver Island, B.C., late 19th cent. *Mechanical type:* represents a large supernatural being known as Crooked Beak of the Sky. It is one of many complex articulated faces which were used in the Hamatsa ritual which is a dramatization of a journey by a novice into the realm of great and all-powerful spirits. The large mouth opens and closes by means of strings; its sharp, clacking sound reverberates through the performance area. The smaller faces with hooked noses appear to be purely decorative.

Courtesy Milwaukee Public Museum, Wisconsin.

Plate 13 SECRET SOCIETY MASK

Kwakiutl, northern Vancouver Island, B.C., middle 20th cent. *Mechanical type:* an unusual example that reveals the lengths to which the carvers go in order to create striking, fearsome and novel forms. The mask was used in a secret society ritual in Fort Rupert in the early 1940's. The large beaked creatures are characters residing in the house of a supernatural spirit. The face on the lower right is Crooked Beak, the others are ravens. Since it weighs in excess of 40 pounds and is over five feet in length, the performer must be harnessed into the mask. Ropes are used to secure it to his shoulders. The performer articulates all the beaks at once. This mask was carved by George Wa'kus, Blunden Harbor.

Courtesy Denver Art Museum, Colorado.

Plate 14 SECRET SOCIETY MASK

Kwakiutl, northern Vancouver Island, B.C., early 20th cent. *Mechanical type:* identified as a raven mask used in a secret society ritual. The lower beak can be operated by pulling strings and provides a resounding clacking sound. The long strands of cedar bark help hide the performer's body.

Courtesy Museum of Anthropology, University of British Columbia, Vancouver, B.C.

Plate 15 SECRET SOCIETY MASK

Kwakiutl, Vancouver Island, B.C., late 19th cent.
Mechanical type: worn in a secret society ritual, the
wolf face sits on the performer's head rather than
covering the face. The skull, also carved from wood,
may either be of a stationary type or set on a spring
so that the motion of the performer makes the skull
shake from side to side, suggesting a state of frenzy.

*Courtesy Museum of the American Indian,
New York.*

Plate 16 FAMILY CREST MASK

Kwakiutl, northern Vancouver Island, B.C., probably late 19th cent. *Mechanical type:* several feet in length with many movable parts. The body representing a killer whale sits on the performer's head; the flukes may be made to rise and fall; the ventral fins move from side to side and the mouth can be opened and closed. In some masks of this type the large dorsal fins disappear into a cavity hollowed in the body, then spring up providing additional surprises for the audience.

Courtesy Museum of Anthropology, University of British Columbia, Vancouver.

Plate 17 FAMILY CREST MASK

Kwakiutl, northern Vancouver Island, B.C., late 19th cent. *Single face type:* a massive, fleshy face symbolizing the octopus who rules the ocean. Notice the many variations of this sea monster conceived by carvers. Sucker cup disks cover the face and forehead. The hole in the top of the mask may have held an animal or bird which is now missing.

Courtesy Museum of Anthropology, University of British Columbia, Vancouver, B.C.

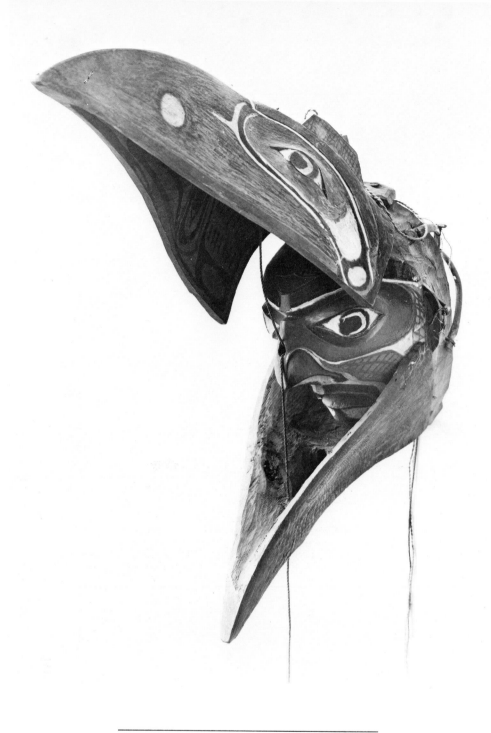

Plate 18 FAMILY CREST MASK

Kwakiutl, northern Vancouver Island, B.C., late 19th cent. *Transformation mask:* an example of the bird-into-human being transformation used in the enactment of many dramas. The outer face represents a raven, an important mythological hero. When open it reveals a human face which might represent the ancestor. These masks express the duality of living creatures and their ability to change outward forms at will.

Courtesy Field Museum of Natural History, Chicago.

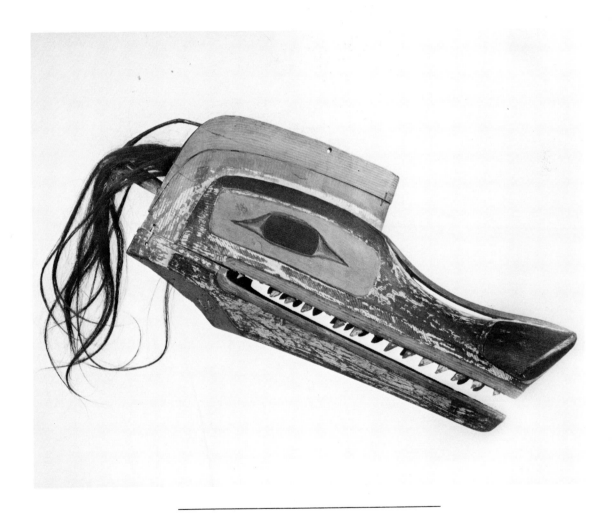

Plate 19 SECRET SOCIETY MASK

Nootka, western Vancouver Island, B.C., late 18th cent. *Single face type:* a mask worn on the forehead rather than over the face and representing a wolf. It was used in a secret society rite called the Wolf Dance, during which initiates enact their capture by the wolf people and bestowal of special powers upon them before they are released. Wolves were considered to be important benefactors among the Nootka tribes and were admired for their wisdom and courage.

Courtesy Denver Art Museum, Colorado.

Plate 20 FAMILY CREST MASK

Kwakiutl, northern Vancouver Island, B.C., early 20th cent. *Single face type:* the central face represents a killer whale with large dorsal fin projecting upwards from the forehead. It is surrounded by a large, flat corolla with painted symbols representing the sun's rays and hands. The mask is called "Killer Whale on the Sun" and represents the acquisition of two crests from different inherited sources as the possession of one family.

Courtesy Milwaukee Public Museum, Wisconsin.

Plate 21   FAMILY CREST MASK

Kwakiutl, northern Vancouver Island, B.C., late 19th cent. *Single face type: a variation of Komokwa, the giant octopus who rules the undersea.* While sucker cups are missing on this mask the large object on the head represents the starfish. There are six curved rays each with a length of about twelve inches. The eyebrows are made of copper.

Courtesy Museum of Anthropology, University of British Columbia, Vancouver, B.C.

Plate 22 SECRET SOCIETY MASK

Bella Coola, central British Columbia, late 19th cent. *Single face type:* face with hawk nose identifies it as a sun mask. The five ornate projections represent the sun's rays. Masks of this type were used in some secret society dances such as the kusiut but it may also represent a family crest.

Courtesy Museum of Anthropology, University of British Columbia, Vancouver, B.C.

Plate 23 FAMILY CREST MASK

Kwakiutl, northern Vancouver Island, B.C., early 20th cent. *Single face type:* represents the Bukwis, wild man. Masks of this type were used in winter ceremonies. It is believed that the woods are inhabited by wild men, people who are eccentric in behavior, or bewitched, pathetic creatures roaming the forest. It is not known what the four horizontal bars across the face represent.

Courtesy Vancouver Centennial Museum, Vancouver, B.C.

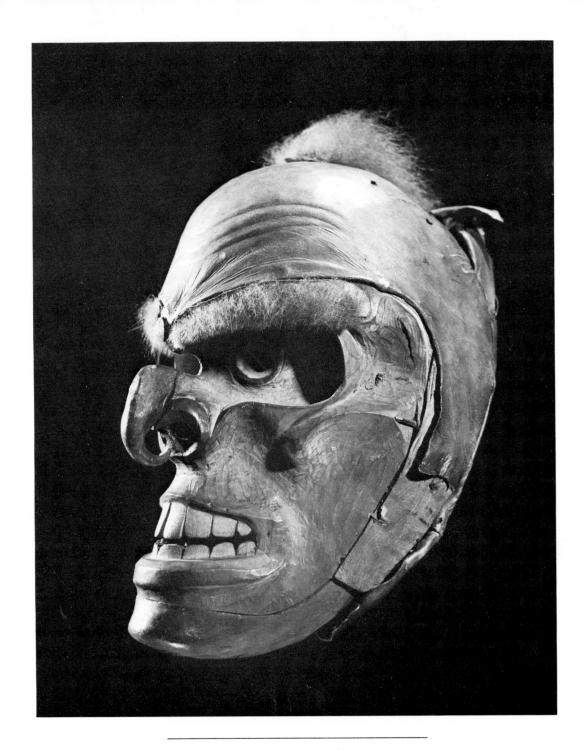

Plate 24 FAMILY CREST MASK

Kwakiutl, northern Vancouver Island, B.C., late 19th cent. *Single face type:* a variation of the mask seen in Plate 23, but with more frightening features. The bukwis or wild men had formerly been residents of a particular village, but through neglect of taboos or through interference from a spirit, lost their sanity and became wild. While this mask has a fearful countenance, it is said Bukwis were generally passive and would not molest others unless attempts were made to rescue them. The mask was displayed in the winter dances.

Courtesy Milwaukee Public Museum, Wisconsin.

Plate 25 FAMILY CREST MASK

Kwakiutl, northern Vancouver Island, B.C., early
20th cent. *Transformation mask:* the upper figure is
that of a crane. Its long neck is in three segmented
parts and strings can pull it erect. The beak can be
opened and closed and the head turned from side to
side. The wings (bare in this photograph) are also
stringed and segmented. In actual use they were
covered with cloth, simulating wings. Pulling the
strings together made both wings fly open, revealing
an anthropomorphic face, probably another rendering
of Komokwa.

Courtesy Denver Art Museum, Colorado.

Plates 26A & 26B FAMILY CREST MASK

Kwakiutl, Vancouver Island, B.C., early 20th cent.
Transformation mask: large outside face (A) represents a thunderbird. The strings pull apart the four hinged sections (B) and reveal another important tribal crest, the double-headed serpent (left and right painted sides) and the central face of this creature. Notice the hinges of leather nailed to the wood, and the appenage (A) which provides the leverage for opening the mask. Split-second timing is of great importance in the opening and closing of such complex masks for dramatic effect.

Courtesy Denver Art Museum, Colorado.

Plates 27A & 27B FAMILY CREST MASK

Kwakiutl, northern Vancouver Island, B.C., late 19th cent. *Transformation mask:* the outer mask (A) is in the form of a raven as a fabulous, mythic bird. It is in excess of three feet in length. Notice the small wooden arm which extends from the side of the mask, the means by which the mask opens. The outer face breaks into four parts and reveals a human face which, however, represents the double-headed serpent, another mythic creature and important family crest (B). The serpent's heads are painted on the insides of the raven's beak and head. Notice the position of the strings above the forehead of the serpent face and the base of the chin. Decorative designs within the mask are often as important as those depicted on the outside.

Courtesy Museum of Anthropology, University of British Columbia, Vancouver, B.C.

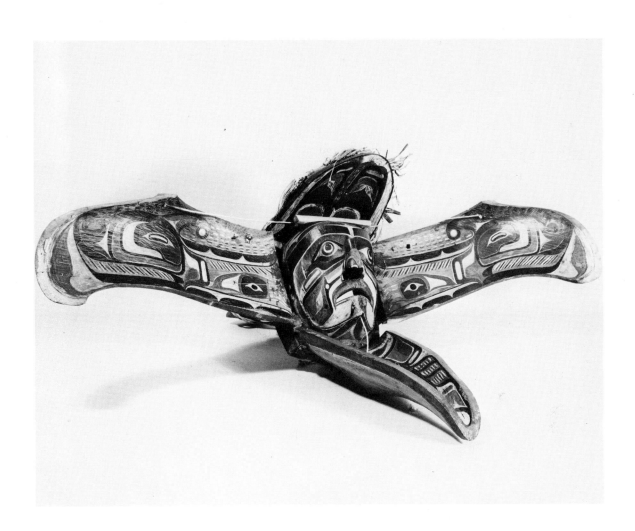

Plate 28 FAMILY CREST MASK

Kwakiutl, northern Vancouver Island, B.C., late 19th
cent. *Transformation mask:* the outer mask may represent *another variant of Komokwa*, the octopus.
The inner face is the human counterpart of the sea
monster. Atop the mask is a sea gull which can be
made to revolve. The design inside the outer face appears to be purely decorative.

*Courtesy Museum of the American Indian,
New York.*

Plate 29 RIDICULE MASK

Kwakiutl, northern Vancouver Island, B.C., late 19th cent. *Single face type:* lineage chiefs often fought each other for coveted tribal positions through the medium of the potlatch. This mask represents a chief in the process of being humiliated by the wealth of his host. One of the ways wealth was conspicuously consumed among the Kwakiutl was by throwing costly eulachon oil over the fire causing intense heat. Rather than lose face before his tribe, a rival would stay in his place. Slowly the fire burns away the side of his face; the potlatch host has triumphed.

Courtesy Field Museum of Natural History, Chicago.

Plate 30   FAMILY CREST MASK

Kwakiutl, northern Vancouver Island, B.C., late 19th-early 20th cent. *Transformation mask:* the long, slender outer face is that of a wolf. Strings attached to the eyes pull the face apart into two equal parts, revealing a raven's face. Its beak opens and closes. The inside of the wolf head is painted with free-form lines. Such masks are startling in semi-darkness as first one creature then another appears.

Courtesy American Museum of Natural History, New York.

Plate 31 FAMILY CREST MASK

Kwakiutl, northern Vancouver Island, B.C., late 19th cent. *Mechanical type:* represents an octopus. The upper face is that of a loon, the solitary bird of the wilderness. It has a movable neck and beak that can swing from right to left. The lower face represents the ruler of the sea.

Courtesy American Museum of Natural History, New York.

Plate 32 FAMILY CREST MASK

Kwakiutl, northern Vancouver Island, B.C., early
20th cent. *Single face type:* a small mask known as
Gikumlth, representing the wild woman of the forests
whose name is Tzo-no-qua. She is an important tribal
crest and is often seen in mask form when a host at a
potlatch wishes to signal that the giving away of property has come to an end.

*Courtesy American Museum of Natural History,
New York.*

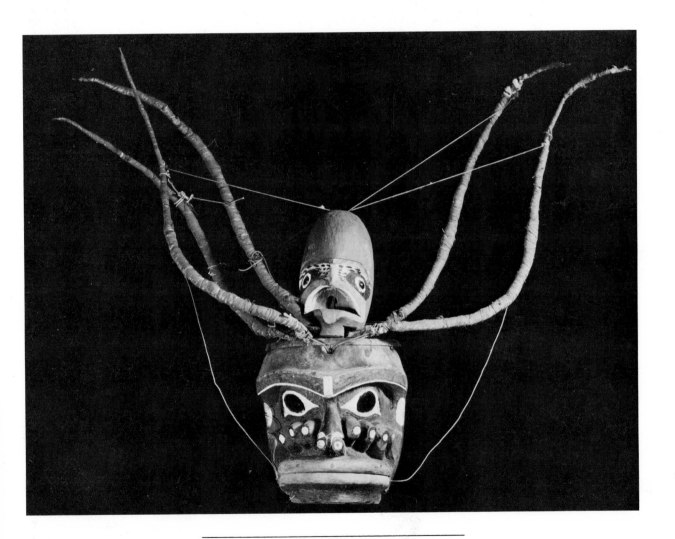

Plate 33 FAMILY CREST MASK

Kwakiutl, northern Vancouver Island, B.C., late 19th cent. *Mechanical type:* the mask represents the giant octopus; its great tentacles can be manipulated by strings which cannot be easily discerned in the firelight. The larger face has sucker cups across the cheeks and a mouth which opens and closes.

Courtesy American Museum of Natural History, New York.

Plate 34 SECRET SOCIETY MASK

Bella Coola, central British Columbia, late 19th cent.
Single face type: an atypical mask from this region
said to represent Grouse who watches over the winter
dances. No other data. Crudely made with little real
carving skill exhibited, it seems more like the fun
masks the Kwakiutl often used in play-potlatching
activities.

*Courtesy American Museum of Natural History,
New York.*

Plate 35   FACE MASK

Nootka, southwest Vancouver Island, B.C., late 19th cent. *Single face type:* represents the Nootka version of the wild man of the forests and it is used in winter dances. The face and hair are of red cedar bark and feathers. Its stark white face gives a frightening, other-world quality to its countenance.

Courtesy American Museum of Natural History, New York.

Plate 36 SECRET SOCIETY MASK

Nootka, southern Vancouver Island, B.C., middle 19th cent. *Mechanical type:* a rare type with two separate faces hinged together and having slotted appendages. These can be opened and closed accordian-fashion. The animal face may represent a wolf but Boas identifies such faces as Hin Emix, a fabulous bird-being. The lower face has eyes and mouth which open and close. Nootkan rituals had similarities with the Kwakiutl and may represent borrowings. We know almost nothing about them as the rituals have disappeared and few studies have been made of the masks.

Courtesy American Museum of Natural History, New York.

Plate 37 KWAKIUTL IN DANCING COSTUME

This man was one of several Indians invited to participate in Northwest Coast Indian exhibits during the
Field Columbian World Exposition in Chicago in
1894. The extreme complexity of dancing costume
shown here is characteristic of only two southern
Kwakiutl tribes—from Kingcome Inlet and Blunden
Harbor. The face worn on the head represents a bird,
its wings extending down the arms on either side;
over the chest is the double-headed serpent, an important family crest. The lower abdomen represents the
killer whale with a seal in its mouth. Hanging upside
down beside the seal and killer whale are two skulls
symbolic of the Hamatsa, the so-called Cannibal Society. To date there has been almost no research done
on these unusual costumes.

*Courtesy Field Museum of Natural History,
Chicago.*

Plate 38 FACE MASK, THE SASQUATCH

Coast Salish, Harrison River area, B.C., early 20th cent. *Single face type:* carved alder face of the furry giant of the forest with small round eyes of red cedar. Commercially tanned fur surrounds top of mask with loose fur below. There is no painted surface. The furry giant is a subject of many folk tales. Controversy as to its actual existence exists today.

Courtesy Vancouver Centennial Museum, Vancouver, B.C.

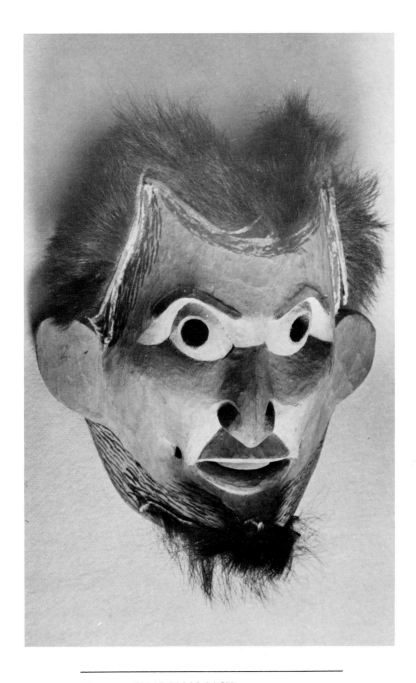

Plate 39 SHAMAN MASK

Bella Coola, central British Columbia, late 19th cent.
Single face type: a human face with little or no surface design. The hair on the head and chin is black
bear fur. The mask is simple, straight forward, realistic; its expression a stark and vacant stare. Little is
known about shaman masks of this tribe.

*Courtesy American Museum of Natural History,
New York.*

Plate 40   SECRET SOCIETY MASK

Bella Coola, central British Columbia, late 19th cent.
Single face type: human-like face that is said to represent the moon. The heavy jowls, thick lips, full nostrils, and projecting eyes are characteristic of this tribal style.

Courtesy Museum of Anthropology, University of British Columbia, Vancouver, B.C.

Plate 41 PORTRAIT MASK

Tsimshian, upper Nass River, B.C., middle to late
19th cent. *Single face type:* a strikingly realistic face
of an aged woman, with hair decoration and elaborate
labret inlaid with abalone shell. Status and rank of
women among northern tribes were shown by the
presence and size of lip plugs. It is most probably a
mask representing a person of extremely high rank
and privilege.

Courtesy Museum of the American Indian,
New York.

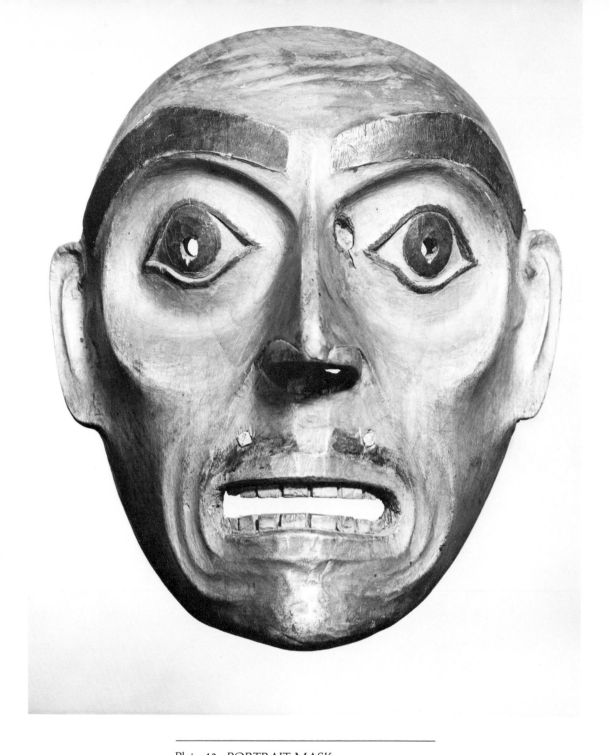

Plate 42 PORTRAIT MASK

Tsimshian, northern British Columbia, late 19th cent.
Single face type: the hollow eyes, sunken cheeks,
tense mouth and empty stare suggests a starving or
emotionally tortured man. It eloquently demonstrates
the skills of the Northwest Coast carvers to capture
nuances of human emotions. The mask may be symbolic or it may represent an actual person.
Courtesy Portland Art Museum, Oregon.

Plate 43 SHAMAN MASK

Tsimshian, northern British Columbia, late 19th cent.
Single face type: represents a ghost. The hollow eyes
and tongue protruding from between the teeth give a
fearful appearance. This mask might have been used
by a shaman in healing rites; such masks often involved communicating with a departed person.

*Courtesy American Museum of Natural History,
New York.*

Plate 44 PORTRAIT MASKS

Haida, Queen Charlotte Islands, B.C., late 19th cent.
Single face types: the lower two appear to be portrait masks representing women, the others men. What these masks were used for is not known, but it is possible they were carved for the tourist trade of the middle and late 19th century. The face in the upper right has markings around the mouth that suggest a sculpin and could symbolize some form of group identity.

Courtesy American Museum of Natural History, New York.

Plate 45 PORTRAIT MASK

Haida, Queen Charlotte Islands, B.C., middle-late 19th cent. *Single face type:* a smaller than life-size face representing a young woman of aristocratic rank. The large labret and dangling abalone shell nose ornament are testimonials of her status, while additional inlay of abalone in cheek and forehead areas symbolize wealth. The mechanically constructed eyes open and close.

Courtesy Provincial Museum, Victoria, B.C.

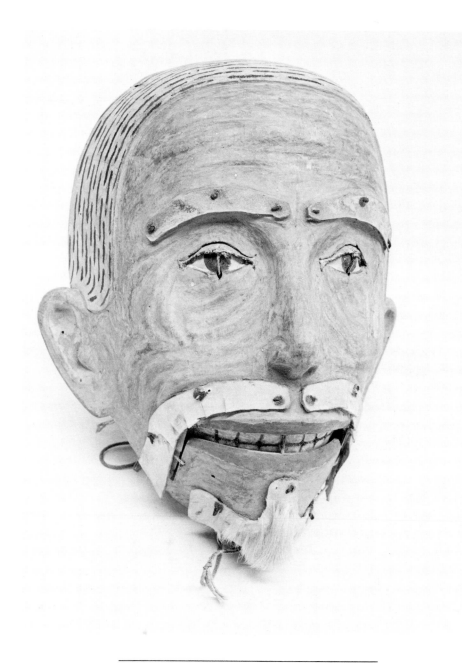

Plate 46   PORTRAIT MASK

Haida, Queen Charlotte Islands, B.C., middle-late 19th cent. *Single face type:* a somewhat smaller than life-sized face probably representing a foreigner or non-Indian. Note the sagging folds of skin on the cheeks and under the eyes as well as the hair styliza-tion. The chin and eyes are movable. Fur strips had decorated the eyebrows, mustache and beard.

Courtesy Provincial Museum, Victoria, B.C.

Plate 47 FACE MASK

Haida, Queen Charlotte Islands, B.C., middle 19th
cent. *Single face type:* mask is said to be used in ceremonial dances and represents the face of a man after
he has encountered a spirit.

*Courtesy American Museum of Natural History,
New York.*

Plate 48 SHAMAN MASK

Haida, Prince of Wales Island, Alaska, late 19th cent.
Single face type: records indicate that this is a dancing mask but shaman used masks in dance rites also.
The eyes open and close with string which are clearly
visible. The mask may be in incomplete form as the
mouth and eyebrows could have accommodated additional parts which are missing.

*Courtesy American Museum of Natural History,
New York.*

Plate 49 SHAMAN MASK

Tlingit, southeast Alaska, late 19th cent. *Single face type:* a powerful face representing a doctor in a trance; the tongue projects through the lips, the eyes are half closed, looking for that which is not to be revealed to ordinary mortals. (Masks of this type do not often have eye holes.) Salvaged from a grave house on Admiralty Island.

Courtesy American Museum of Natural History, New York.

Plate 50   SHAMAN MASK

Tlingit, southeast Alaska, late 19th cent. *Single face type:* an Indian doctor in a curing rite, a common type of mask among the Tlingit. The tongue projects through the lips and possibly represents the trance-like state through which the practitioner is communicating with the spirit world.

Courtesy American Museum of Natural History, New York.

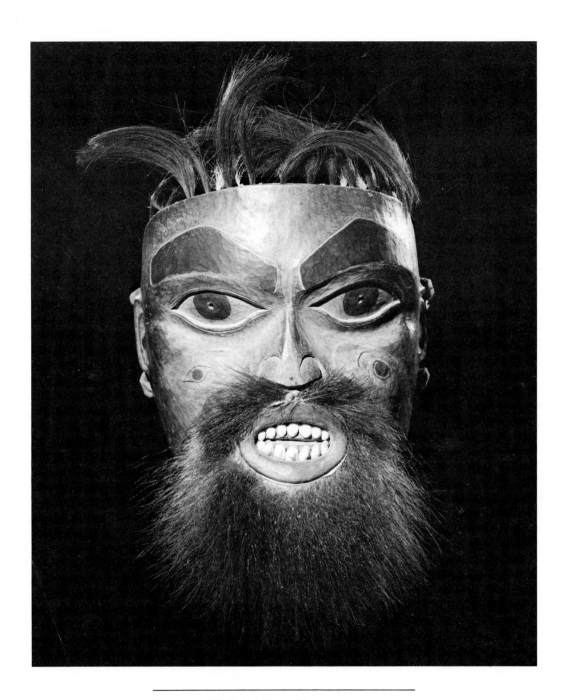

Plate 51 SHAMAN MASK

Tlingit, southeast Alaska, middle to late 19th cent.
Single face type: a striking face used by an Indian
doctor for curing. The mouth is inlaid with opercula
shells, the beard is black bear fur. Tufts of hair on the
head are placed in small holes and held with pegs.
Shaman masks obviously have emotional content but
the exact nature of their use and meaning remain unknown to all but the shaman himself.

*Courtesy American Museum of Natural History,
New York.*

Plate 52   PORTRAIT MASK

Tsimshian, northern British Columbia, late 19th cent.
Single face type: a sensitive masterpiece probably
representing a person honored in a memorial service.
The holes in the upper lip and over the eyes once
held patches of fur for mustache and eyebrows which
have disintegrated. While the wrinkled face is rendered with stylized surface lines, it is a believable
expression of old age.

*Courtesy Museum of the American Indian,
New York.*

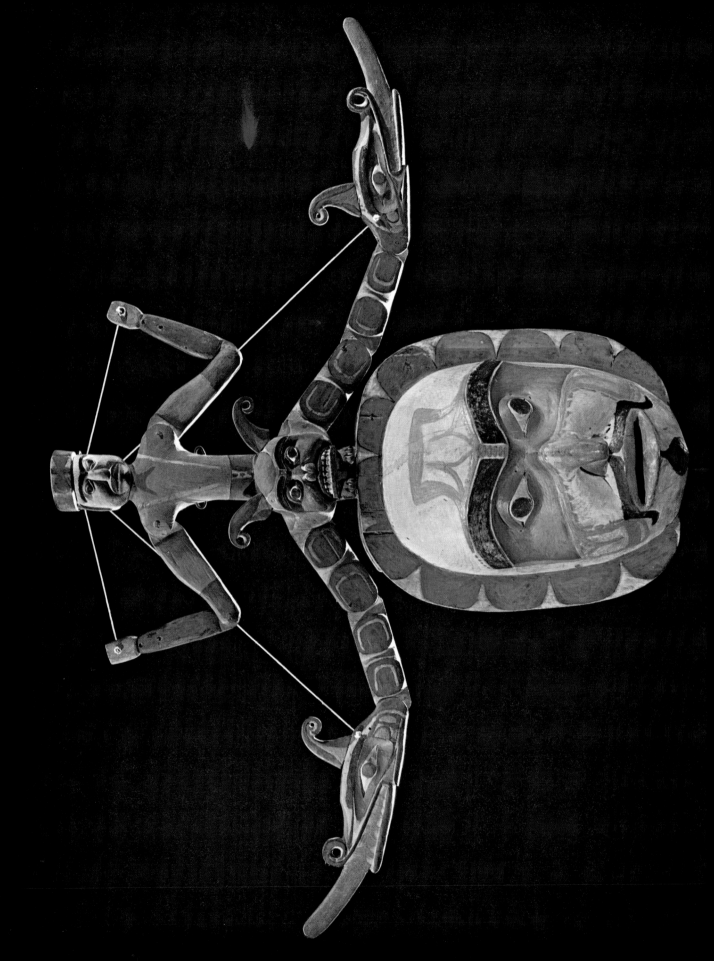

Plate 53 FAMILY CREST MASK

Kwakiutl, northern Vancouver Island, B.C., late 19th cent. *Mechanical type:* a complicated type similar to those in plates 3, 20, 30. The larger face represents the sun with its numerous small circular rays. Just above is the crest of the double-headed serpent, the two extremities with snake-like heads attached to the central face. Above this is a human form with crudely carved movable hands and arms, which in turn move the heads of the serpents.

Courtesy Provincial Museum, Victoria, B.C.

Plate 54 FAMILY CREST MASK

Kwakiutl, northern Vancouver Island, B.C., early 20th cent. *Transformation type:* the outer mask is a larger-than-life face representing Tzo-no-qua, the ogress of the forests. The mask opens revealing a human-like face having little surface decoration. It could represent the spirit's human counterpart or an ancestor who acquired wealth as a result of an encounter with her. Though Tzo-no-qua is a fearsome spirit, she is also held in the highest regard and affection. A crest claimed by most of the illustrious lineages of the Kwakiutl, she is a symbol of eating, food giving, and the acquisition of vast amounts of wealth.

Courtesy Portland Art Museum, Oregon.

Plate 55 PORTRAIT MASK

Tsimshian, northern British Columbia, late 19th-early 20th cent. *Single face type:* a life-size realistic mask representing a handsome young woman. The eyebrows are painted rather than sculpted on the face and designs are painted in red over forehead and cheeks. Attached to the hair are two small bird-like figures which seem to be eagles. The eyes have holes large enough to see through.

Courtesy Portland Art Museum, Oregon.

Plate 56 PORTRAIT MASK

Haida, Queen Charlotte Islands, B.C., middle 19th cent. *Single face type:* this face has a combination of realistic and stylized features. The treatment of the hair, ears and mouth being the former, while stylized elements include the painting around the eyes and the circular designs across the face. These may represent the sun. Animal fur provides the beard and eyebrows. This mask may represent a specific person.

Courtesy Provincial Museum, Victoria, B.C.

ANNOTATED BIBLIOGRAPHY OF REFERENCES

Boas, Franz   *1897*   The Social Organization and Secret Societies of the Kwakiutl Indians. *Report of the U.S. National Museum for 1895, Washington, D.C.*

A complicated but comprehensive description of the ritual and ceremonial life of tribes centered around Fort Rupert, B.C.

1900   The Mythology of the Bella Coola Indians. *Memoirs of the American Museum of Natural History, New York, part II.*

A brief but fascinating description with illustrations of the major mythological themes found among these tribes.

1935   Kwakiutl Culture As Reflected in Mythology. *American Folklore Society, Memoir XXVIII, New York.*

The rich and varied myths which are recurrent in the culture of the people in this region.

1955   Primitive Art. *Dover Publications, New York.*

The first comprehensive analysis of Northwest Coast Indian art written by the pioneer of such studies and worth reading and rereading.

Codere, Helen   *1950*   Fighting With Property. *Monographs of the American Ethnological Society, J.J. Augustin, N.Y. Vol. XVIII.*

A comprehensive historically-oriented analysis of the origin and development of the Kwakiutl potlatching system.

Dockstader, Frederick   *1961*   Indian Art In America. *New York Graphic Society, Greenwich, Conn.*

A general book on the art of American Indian lavishly illustrated; excellent examples of Northwest Coast art pieces.

Duff, Wilson   *1964*   The Indian History of British Columbia: The Impact of the White Man. *Queen's Printer, Victoria, Vol. 1, memoir 5.*

A scholarly, in-depth analysis of the effects of white settlement and penetration among the Northwest Coast tribes in the nineteenth century.

Feder, Norman
  & Edward Malin   *1962*   Indian Art of the Northwest Coast. *Denver Art Museum, Winter Quarterly.*

An overview of the main features of Northwest Indian art including a description of the cultural background.

Garfield, Viola   *1955*   Making a Bird or Chief's Rattle. *Davidson Journal of Anthropology, Seattle. Winter, Vol. 1, No. 2.*

A description of the step-by-step techniques a Tsimshian carver used in the making of a ceremonial object.

Garfield, Viola
  & Paul Wingert   *1965*   The Tsimshian Indians and Their Arts. *University of Washington Press, Seattle.*

Two scholarly professionals, one in ethnography, the other in art history, analyze the characteristics of Tsimshian culture.

Gunther, Erna   *1966*   Art in the Life of the Northwest Coast Indians. *Portland Art Museum, Portland, Oregon.*

A justly famous leader in the recognition of Northwest Coast art as great art shares her deep and comprehensive knowledge of the famed Rasmussen collection.

Holm, Bill   *1972*   Heraldic Carving Styles of the Northwest Coast, in American Indian Art: Form and Function. *Minneapolis Institute of Arts.*

A brief but succinct review of major features of Northwest sculpture written by an expert in the field.

Holm, Bill
  & Bill Reid   1975   Form and Freedom. *Institute for the Arts, Rice University, Houston.*

A dialog between two gifted individuals, an Indian and a white, about specific objects in a major art collection in the United States.

Hawthorn, Audrey 1964   Mungo Martin: Artist and Craftsman. *Beaver Magazine, Winnipeg.*

A brief description of this Kwakiutl artist with painted illustrations of creatures who he envisioned inhabited his world. Very worthwhile reading and thinking about.

              1967   Art of the Kwakiutl Indians. *University of Washington Press, Seattle and London.*

A good introductory text profusely illustrated in color and black and white photographs of the range of aesthetic arts of these tribal groups; the major part of the collection illustrated is derived from early to middle twentieth century sources.

Hawthorn, Harry   The Artist in Tribal Society: The Northwest Coast, *in the book* The Artist in Tribal Society *edited by Marion Smith, The Free Press, Glencoe.*

An analysis of the working habits and techniques of Mungo Martin, the Kwakiutl carver, as seen in a context removed from his native village and environs.

Kuh, Katharine 1971   The First Americans As Artists. *Saturday Review, September 4 issue.*

A highly provocative article calling the reader's attention to the indifference, neglect, and despair of the Native American arts in Alaska and British Columbia.

Laguna,
 Frederica de   1972   Under Mt. Saint Elias: The History and Culture of the
                              Yakutat Tlingit. *Smithsonian Institution Press,
                              Washington, D.C. 3 volumes.*

                              *An exceedingly detailed description and analysis of a
                              little-known Tlingit group in the northern periphery of
                              the Northwest Coast, accompanied by a large selection
                              of photographs of both people and arts taken when the
                              group was viable and intact. A valuable resource tool
                              for any study of Northwest Coast Indians.*

La Violette, F.E.   1961   The Struggle for Survival: Indian Cultures and the
                              Protestant Ethic in British Columbia. *University of
                              Toronto Press, Toronto.*

                              *A scholarly study pinpointing the details behind the
                              legislative and missionary points of view resulting in
                              the undermining and collapse of Indian institutions in
                              British Columbia. Heavy reading but should not be
                              missed.*

Malin, Edward   1946-49   Unpublished Field Notes From Fort Rupert and Alert
                              Bay Villages.

                     1969   The Seal and Salmon Indians: The Koskimo Kwakiutl of
                              Northern Vancouver Island. *Unpublished manuscript
                              dealing with Kwakiutl groups in Quatsino Inlet.*

Mochon, Marion J.   1966   Masks of the Northwest Coast: The Samuel A. Barrett
                              Collection, *Milwaukee Public Museum, publications in
                              primitive art, #2.*

                              *A valuable addition to the literature dealing with
                              masks and other ceremonial materials from the central
                              coastal region of British Columbia. Every interested
                              person should have the opportunity to become familiar
                              with its contents.*

MacNair, Peter   1973-74   Kwakiutl Winter Dances: A Reenactment. *Arts Canada
                              Magazine, Toronto.*

                              *A brief article with exceptional photographs of some of
                              the Kwakiutl dances performed during a recent
                              potlatch in which an Indian celebrity played host.*

McDonald, George 1972   Ksan: Breath of Our Grandfathers. *National Museums of Canada, Ottawa.*

A short commentary and introduction to the revival of carving arts among the many gifted Tsimshian carvers. While the masks illustrated are contemporary they illustrate that the skills and controls in wood sculpture have not been lost. The Grandfathers may look with extreme satisfaction on what the people are doing at Ksan.

McFeat, T. *(editor)* 1967   Indians of the North Pacific Coast. *University of Washington Press, Seattle.*

A series of articles compiled by the editor which have a great deal of merit. Includes a few authored by Indians. It is a handy paperback to carry about while traveling on the Coast.

McIlwraith, T.F. 1948   The Bella Coola Indians. *University of Toronto Press, Toronto. 2 volumes.*

The scope and breadth of the investigator's ethnological researchers make these volumes stand in a class by themselves. Most of what is written has long since passed from the scene of Bella Coola descendants in Canada.

Vancouver
Art Gallery 1967   Arts of the Raven: Masterworks by the Northwest Coast Indian. *Bergthorson & Derreth, Vancouver.*

Worthwhile articles by Duff, Holm, and Reid accompany many illustrations in color and black and white photographs of this pace-setting special exhibit honoring British Columbia's Indian heritage.

Waite, Deborah 1966   Kwakiutl Transformation Masks. *In The Many Faces of Primitive Art, edited by Douglas Fraser, Prentice-Hall, New Jersey.*

An introductory study of this very complex subject, briefly analyzed and described but worth reading. Illustrations are just fair but give the reader insights to pursue the subject in greater detail.

Wingert, Paul   *1962*   Primitive Art: Its Styles and Traditions. *Oxford University Press, New York.*

While this book focuses only briefly on Northwest Coast art and centers rather on African and Oceanic sculpture, it is a very valuable tool for the concepts described here. Wingert was a wide-ranging art historian and what he writes about is worth the reader's attention.

Plate 57

A. George Nelson (Si-wiss), a Koskimo Indian from Vancouver Island, begins to carve a mask of a sea spirit who is known as Ya-ghis. The block of wood is red cedar, the elbow adze being used to strip away the basic shape is of traditional form.
Photo by author taken in 1950.

B. Nelson has cut away the extraneous wood and the face is revealed. He begins to cut out the details with crooked and straight knives. He is here using a straight-bladed knife, cutting with movements towards him rather than away from him. In this way he controls the blade and the amount of wood to be removed with much greater precision.
Photo by author.

C. The face of Ya-ghis is revealed. Nelson now paints the final details of teeth and nose. The inside of the mask is hollowed out before painting begins. Paints are of commercial hardware variety. The mask took two days to complete.
Photo by author.

A ROSTER OF MODERN MASK CARVERS
FROM THE NORTHWEST COAST

NAME	TRIBE	RESIDENCE OR AFFILIATION
George Benson	Tlingit	Sitka, Alaska
Nathan Jackson	Tlingit	Haines, Alaska
Leo Jacobs	Tlingit	Haines, Alaska
Amos Wallace	Tlingit	Juneau, Alaska
Lincoln Wallace	Tlingit	Hoonah, Alaska
Robert Davidson	Haida	Skidegate, Q.C.I.
Bill Reid	Haida	Vancouver, B.C.
Norman Tait	Tsimshian	Unknown
Roy Vickers	Tsimshian	Unknown
Abel Campbell	Tsimshian	Ksan Village, B.C.
Freda Diesing	Haida	Ksan Village, B.C.
Leonard Duncan	Tsimshian	Ksan Village, B.C.
Herb Green	Tsimshian	Ksan Village, B.C.
Murphy Green	Tsimshian	Ksan Village, B.C.
Walter Harris	Tsimshian	Ksan Village, B.C.
Doreen Jensen	Tsimshian	Ksan Village, B.C.
Alfred Joseph	Tsimshian	Ksan Village, B.C.
Victor Mowatt	Tsimshian	Ksan Village, B.C.
Earl Muldoe	Tsimshian	Ksan Village, B.C.
Murphy Stanley	Tsimshian	Ksan Village, B.C.
Vernon Stephens	Tsimshian	Ksan Village, B.C.
Art Sterritt	Tsimshian	Ksan Village, B.C.
Douglas Cranmer	Kwakiutl	Alert Bay, B.C.
Jimmy Dick	Kwakiutl	Alert Bay, B.C.
Charlie George	Kwakiutl	Alert Bay, B.C.
Dick Hawkins	Kwakiutl	Alert Bay, B.C.
Joe Sewid	Kwakiutl	Alert Bay, B.C.
Louis Sewid	Kwakiutl	Alert Bay, B.C.
Calvin Hunt	Kwakiutl	Arts of Raven Gallery, Victoria
Henry Hunt	Kwakiutl	Arts of Raven Gallery, Victoria
Tony Hunt	Kwakiutl	Arts of Raven Gallery, Victoria
Joe David	Nootka	Unknown

COLOPHON
This book was designed by Chas. S. Politz of the
Design Council, Inc., set in eleven point Paladium
by Metro-Portland Typesetting, lithographed by
Moore Lithograph Company and bound by Lincoln
and Allen, Inc., Portland, Oregon.